To Doc Chapman

You have seen the birch logs
burning and have heard
the long cry of the loon,
The Hinabashoo on
the night wind has
spoken to you of
far away places —
Good Canoeing
Carle W. Handel
7/11/'55

CANOE CAMPING

a guide to wilderness travel

CANOE CAMPING

a guide to wilderness travel

Carle Walker Handel
illustrated by
G. Fred Schueler

A. S. Barnes and Company
New York

IN APPRECIATION

When you catch a whiff of wood smoke, see the haze on the hills, hear the geese high in the sky or a train whistle far away in the night, there come crowding a thousand memories of a thousand nights under the stars over thousands of miles of trail, and that deep vibrant urge rises up within you to be up and off to faraway places. So it will be, to the end of your days, as long as physical energy, sight, hearing, and smell shall last. Your memory's ear will hear always the hurried pad of moccasined feet, the creak of pack leather, the chunking of the paddle, the canoeing songs little known to civilized man, and the whisper of the Wina-Ba-Shoo on the night wind in the pines as you are lulled to sleep on a bed of fragrant balsam.

In a span of over forty years in the open and on the trail, the author has become indebted to many for his accumulated knowledge of nature lore, but here he can express his appreciation only to a few of the hundreds at whose feet was accomplished the humble and, at times, painful art of learning, which helped to forge the contents of this book. Many of these people were graduates of universities, many others had never seen more than a two-story building and could only make a blaze or a mark to indicate their names, but all contributed.

My mother, whose deep love of the out-of-doors guided her son on a quest for knowledge of those things which God shows to us in the pages of nature, and whose deep understanding and guidance has been, and always will be, a deep motivating inspiration.

My father, by whose side I sat on the buckboard behind the horses in the dawn and at sunset, as he told and showed me the ways of courage and fortitude that become a man.

To my lovely wife Dorothy, who has paddled unexplored rivers with me and has been an unfailing companion at all times on the long trail, whether in the wilderness or on the sometimes rugged pathway of life, and who is now helping to start George and Susan along the way to new trails in an unknown future; whose only shield often is the unfaltering faith of the explorer in God and his own courage.

To my brother Paul, who has shared so much with me on the trail, and whose superb woodcraft is unparalleled.

To my brother George, with whom I have fished and waded the streams, learning much from him of the riddles of the finny art.

To my younger brother Neil, who now explores deep into the field of science, and who once demonstrated his marksmanship by snuffing a candle first at twenty paces without touching the wick.

To Robert Spinks, our caretaker, who, drawing upon his experiences as a soldier, canal-boater, and woodsman, inspired my brothers and me with his woods, fishing and hunting lore. His yarns to three small boys by the smoky light of an oil lamp, while the rain drummed on the tin roof at the farm are unforgettable.

To Byron Winn, Scoutmaster, whose understanding ways helped build dreams of boys into deeds of men.

To Hermann Bauman, Scout executive, whose deep love of the pioneer, the Indian, nature and the lore of the woods opened the doors of exploration to me and to thousands of now-responsible citizens during his thirty years as our local Scout executive. A visit to his beautiful home of retirement in the woods where he and Betty, his lovely wife, now live is a constant inspiration.

To Ben Jones, philosopher, teacher, historian, woodsman and "Patriarch of the Hills," who at seventy years trod the hills with us boys, and who, when we sat around the fire or lay rolled in our blankets, taught us a thousand unforgettable things of the frontier and the pioneer

To mention all would fill a book, but among the other men—of all races—at whose feet the author has sat and learned, those who must be mentioned are:

Phil Paquette and Oscar Boyer—Couriers du bois, guides, explorers, trappers, and hunters.
Cal Oswin (English-Canadian), guide; Joe Sutherland (Eskimo), John Mackey (Finlander)
Joe Friday, John Turner
John Wabsquaw, Mike Osogwin (Indians)
Joe and John Boisneau (Bushmen of mixed blood)

There are many others, including Dr. Tom Marsh, George Butterfield, Earl Kelly, Clayton Barr, Kearney Hinsperger, Fee Devine, Frank Luce (guide, hunter and dog trainer), Harold Pierce (life long friend who has panned gold in the Yukon and with whom I have shared many unforgettable experiences including living with a bear for three days) and Sisk (for his inimitable meals on the Algoma Central and Hudson's Bay Railroad for many years). Indian, Eskimo, Finlander, Swede, Norwegian, English, Canadian, American, Irish, Scotch, Negro, Mexican—all contributed to that ever-developing of my knowledge of nature lore. I merely record in this book what they have passed on to me in that hardy, close fellowship along the trail.

Also, among those from the "Halls of Ivy" who have gone into the bush, I must thank Dr. Charles Anspach (College President and fishing buddy), Dr. Frank J. Wright (geologist and scientist), and Dr. A. W. Lindsey (biologist and master scientist), whose teaching reached far beyond books and deep into nature itself.

Special appreciation must be accorded to:

The Honorable George Craig—The Hudson's Bay Company
Hugh Grey—Editor of *Field & Stream*
Albert Bonillia—Rancher and explorer, from Mexico
Capt. Fred C. Mills (retired)—Boy Scouts of America
Gunnar Berg—Boy Scouts of America
William C. Wessel (deceased)—Boy Scouts of America
L. L. McDonald (retired)—Boy Scouts of America
Ernest Thompson Seton
Horace Kephart

FOREWORD

Deep in the hearts of all sportsmen is the dream of a wilderness trip, an expedition that will give them the opportunity to follow the water trails and portages of the voyageurs and relive, at least in part, those days when a man would fill his food pack with a bag of flour, salt, fat bacon and tea, and set out for a many weeks' trip into the bush, confident in his ability to live off the land and return to civilization in better shape than when he left. For most of us these days, however, such a primitive trip would be one of hardship and privation. When we came out, we'd probably be better fitted for a hospital or rest home than a return to our jobs in a soft and indulgent civilization. But any of us can take that wilderness trip if he uses common sense in planning and organization and gears his travels to his capabilities.

Here, between the covers of this book, Carle Handel tells you how to plan such a trip and how to enjoy it. Because he is an experienced woodsman and bush traveler as well as a meticulous planner, Carle has been able to organize and set down those essentials to successful and enjoyable bush travel in such a concise manner that anyone, even the most inexperienced, should be able to plan a successful and enjoyable wilderness trip. Carle's book is the open sesame for thousands upon thousands of sportsmen who have longed to travel back beyond, but had only a vague idea of how to go about it. And like those iron men who hit the bush with only the bare essentials, they will come back to their workaday life not only in tip-top physical shape, but better fitted mentally to cope with the strains and complexities of modern living.

Hugh Grey
Editor, *Field and Stream*

CONTENTS

ILLUSTRATIONS

CANOE CAMPING

a guide to wilderness travel

chapter 1

HIGH ADVENTURE STILL LIVES

We sat around the fire, using a candle in a tin bucket for a light, and pored over a blueprint map. All day we had worked our way through a lake for over twenty calculated miles, taking advantage of islands, headlands and cliffs, sitting in the lee of rocky islands to wait for the strong headwind to let up a little so that we could make the open passages. Then, quartering into wind tandem so that the others would have the advantage of the "slick" of the lead canoe, which would break the sharp edges of the three-foot waves, we had carefully made our way toward the end of the big lake, anxiously watching the sky and mountaintops for weather signs. We had kept track of bays, islands, landmarks, hills and wind direction; we had checked our compass regularly, using the age-old navigation trick of looking back at regular intervals to check our "wind drift" and "headway."

Anyone who has traveled the "bush country"—or in fact, any wild country—knows that a sense of direction depends on keeping one's eyes and ears open and being sensitive to signs along the way, to any change of direction; one must "hindsight" regularly so as to know what the trail looks like should it be necessary to backtrack. Other helps are the compass, the direction of the sun, one's shadow, the direction of the wind and current streaks on the water; even a flock of merganser fish ducks over to the left, nose into the wind, their beaks pointing its source like the needles of a floating-dial compass.

With our maps fastened under a couple of pack straps and oriented with a compass tied on top with a string, the other end of which was fastened to the gunnel, we had worked down to the bay from which issued the outlet of the lake. But upon arriving at this bay, we were perplexed at not seeing that telltale break in the skyline which usually indicates the outlet of a large lake.

Several small bays were then skirted, with no success. To the west a mountain rose a sheer thousand feet like a huge fortress wall, defying human efforts to pass it. It was late, so we chose a campsite on a shelving rocky island. (Sand beaches are usually to be avoided in July since they contain more biting pests at that season than do rocky surfaces.) We made camp; beds of balsam were built on which were pitched the two wedge tents of the party, and the beds were laid on the canvas floor of the tents. One canoe went out with instructions to troll with a copper line and an archer spinner over an evident shoal lying between our island and one about a mile to the northwest. The shelving of both islands indicated a glacial scour and a shoal lying one hundred feet or more beneath the surface. And two loons denoted the presence of shiners, sometimes called pin herring, which are the nature food for lake trout. As we had expected, the canoe trip out and back produced two lake trout, twenty pounds in all, for supper and breakfast, the trout being brought back with the usual "fish" stories that accompany such incidents of wilderness life.

With four motions of the hunting knife, each trout was filleted and skinned. The pink meat was chunked and dropped into a pot of boiling salted water on the fire, where, along with a slice of good old raw onion, it was cooked for three minutes. The shredded potatoes also took three minutes to cook, dried spinach the same. Bannock, tea, and applesauce made from dried apples completed a very good meal.

By the time the canoes were up, food cached, extra wood brought in and dishes washed, it was time for the corporation meeting or, in other words, time to talk over the day—to discuss problems, swap stories and smoke.

This night, however, the problem of finding the outlet of the lake was the major topic. The blueprint indicated that we were in the bay outlet to the river, but every landmark visible to us seemed to indicate otherwise. It was explained that practically all maps in wilderness country are designed to give only a general lay of land, lakes and rivers. After digging out the map case from one of the packs, we found there a geological map that had been made of this section of the country and which was more accurate than the regular maps. It showed in many respects a marked variance with the blueprint, but it showed also that the river flowed out of this particular bay. After an hour's discussion, the candle burned out and one by one tired travelers retreated to the blankets.

Finally the guide and I were the only ones left by the fire. After we each had a cup of tea, we walked down to the lake's edge. The wind had long since died, the stars had come out in the brilliant dome overhead, and the ghostly flickers of the northern lights were just beginning down under the Big Dipper and Cassiopeia. We stood on the shore a long time. A white-throated sparrow's sleepy song drifted over the water, a sweet interlude in that great silence.

Then suddenly it came—a sound, at first like a faint whisper, then louder, then fading out only to arise again, a sound like the distant exhaust of steam or the whispering of a breeze in a Norway pine. The guide's hand pressured my arm as we both listened intently. We knew what it was. From the southwest, under the brow of the mountain, it came—the unmistakable noise of rapids, perhaps a mile or two away. We had found the passage (as we later proved). We rolled into our sleeping bags, knowing that Manitou watches over his children and shows them the way if they are patient and have faith in him.

Thus finding this passage was typical of a thousand experiences in wilderness travel. Many would call it luck, but the wise know that it is based upon a geographical knowledge of one's surroundings. One can derive from certain signs in one's immediate position on the earth's surface a broad general acquaintance with weather, terrain, the stars, and with animal, bird, fish and plant life. The type of rocks and their elevation, the condition of the soil, temperatures, and the amount of snow and rainfall, all create zones of plant and animal life and are a definite influence on any problems the wilderness traveler may find. As this book will deal primarily with "canoe country," we shall not attempt to discuss desert areas; the latter present their own set of problems. Opportunities for hiking, journeying by pack horse and canoeing are great in our own continent. And in the future when, we hope, sportsmen again can travel the vast reaches of Northern Asia and Europe, these opportunities will be even greater.

The many problems confronting wilderness travel in the Northern Hemisphere are similar if one understands the certain basic conditions. First, down to the thirty-eighth parallel in practically all of North America (as well as Europe and Asia), great continental glaciers ground down great mountain ranges (exceptions to this are to be found in the West and Northwest of our continent), leaving a land of topsy-turvy drainage becoming more complex the farther north one travels. Great holes were scooped out, forming literally millions of lakes. Some of the shallower ones filled up with plant life and developed as vast bogs or muskegs (actually a cold coal-forming process of peat moss) which, below the sixtieth parallel, in most instances, became great spruce and cedar swamps, and in the arctic vast tundra bogs. The bones of the continent thrust up through this, as low hills and mountains. In the eastern part of the continent, the Laurentians, the Adirondacks, the New England Shield, the Catskills, the upper Appalachians and the Allegheny chain are the principal ridges. The latter three have been mentioned because there is some truely wild and delightful country to be traveled in these. The Rockies, the Coastal Ranges and their foothills, and the inner basin ranges, also the Black Hills of the West still present a challenge for exploration. The low mountains of the Northwest Territories around the Coppermine, the Great Slave and Great Bear lakes, as well as the Low Iron Bearing Mountains between Ungava and Labrador, are real opportunities to the adventurer who feels the urge to go back beyond. There is much to explore and re-explore. Even the Susquehanna, Delaware, Allegheny, Monongahela, the Upper Mississippi, Missouri, Snake and Columbia rivers, and a host of others, also challenge.

General conditions of physiography foretell, I repeat, some of the traveler's problems, and he should be prepared to meet them.

The latitude, the elevation above sea level, the land mass over which one is traveling, the distance from base of supply at any time during a trip and the opportunity to resupply or the lack of opportunity—all should be taken into consideration. To know what the locale offers in ways of "living off the land" by hunting, fishing, and collecting available wild plant and animal food is important. Data concerning the season of the year and its possible weather conditions—warm or cold, wind, rain, snow, ice or drought—must be assembled and calculated in the manner of that military fine art called "logistics."

If anyone thinks that La Salle, Jacques Cartier, Daniel Boone, Davy Crockett, Jim Bridger, and Lewis and Clark were "just plain lucky," they are far from right. These men survived the wilderness only by profiting from the wisdom and knowledge and the lore gleaned from the trail blazers who went before them, in most cases Indians or Eskimos. La Salle, Boone and others utilized the best-known equipment of the time, and practiced health habits; before adventuring forth they gathered all information possible, as shown by the crude maps which they drew before going and corrected en-route.

The fine art of wilderness travel today is not just for the few, but for the thousands of us who have the blood of our adventuring forefathers flowing through our veins. This is indicated by the vast numbers that take to the "bush" every year in search of adventure. It is for these people—whether they are going to travel the beautiful upper regions of the Delaware or New River or journey to the lonely shores of the Beaufort Sea in the arctic at the top of the Athabaska, Great Slave and McKenzie river system—that I have written this book. Nor is this sport confined to men. Some of the finest canoeists and wilderness travelers that I have known have been women—they make use of skill and knowledge to offset their lack of physical strength in comparison with men. Another point for readers: in many parts of this book, I have mentioned and described the Canadian wilderness when discussing various phases of the craft of wilderness travel, for it is in that area the writer loves to follow the dim trails.

This book, then, is an attempt to describe in simple detail the many aspects of wilderness travel. As illustrated in the beginning of the chapter, even the best preparation will not solve all your problems—and it is this element of the unknown which makes for adventure and fun. At the end of your journey you will be amazed to discover how well Manitou watches over his children.

1. WILLING TEAMMATES
2. PROPER GRUB AND GEAR
3. GOOD GUIDE AND ROUTE
4. READY FOR EMERGENCIES

chapter 2

PLANS AND PREPARATIONS

One of the world's greatest generals once said, "Wars are won or lost on thorough knowledge of the enemy and his country and how well prepared you are to meet both." So it is with a trip into any kind of country. The plans and preparation for a successful "bush trip" consist of the following considerations in their logical sequence:

Selecting Your Traveling Companions
Selecting Your Route
Selecting and Making Ready Your Equipment
Planning and Packing Food and Cooking Gear
Selecting Your Guide
Preparing for Emergencies

SELECTING YOUR TRAVELING COMPANIONS

The first thing to do is to select your companions. Choose people of long acquaintance, whom you know thoroughly. They must be congenial, industrious, willing to undergo discomforts, and must have a love of adventure and the out-of-doors. Avoid foppish people—they don't work out very well on a trip. To be just "good acquaintances" is not enough either, since the small, and hitherto overlooked sins—selfishness, sarcasm, laziness and the like—will become intolerable after living a week in the solitude and toil of the wilderness. *Select your teammates carefully for their kindness toward others, and above all for their natural pride in doing their share of the work and their willingness to help others.* Brothers, these are words of wisdom and mark them well. All who have traveled in the wilderness have seen men do things that are disgusting and tragic because their nerves were rubbed raw by each other. These incidents always causes misery to the others about them. On the other hand, I have seen the wiser ones become friends—a common experience having given them the deep understanding that cements life-long friendships. If you do not think a man will fit in, have the courage to tell him so immediately; he may become a danger to all at a critical moment later on when your very lives depend on his teamwork. So much for the selection of your traveling mates.

After you have made up your "party"—then comes the fun of planning, which will help to measure your friends for what they are worth. This "measuring" process can be a series of very interesting, economical and entertaining evenings and weekends, often for a period of several months. I usually get the travel fever in February or March and I begin to pull out gear, maps, etc., to start the long and pleasant job of getting ready. Plan everything in detail. The women can sew up a new tent. The men can build a new packsack, repair fishing tackle or readjust equipment to strengthen it and eliminate a few extra pounds here and there. Week-end trips can be used to try out your prospective buddies as well as new menus, new cooking gear, tents, mosquito dope and fishing tackle.

Most of all, decide where you are going and heed the following advice: *Travel as light as possible and as comfortable as possible (which is often one and the same thing) but have plenty of grub.* John Wabsquaw, an old Indian, once told me, "White man big fool. Heap big pack, little grub. Indian heap big grub, little pack." Another measure of a good woodsman is that all his gear is inside the pack and that he carries only *one* pack. Quiet-faced men that you will meet on the trail once in a while will look slyly at your outfit, and your entire social standing and respect with them will be dependent on the kind of equipment that you have and how you have taken care of it, above all on whether it has been placed in a few well-selected packsacks or not. They will also look at what you wear and how you wear it. If you are new in the country, it is best to ask for advice, especially about equipment, the trail, portages, short cuts, fish, etc. You will learn much if you remember that the ways of learning are often humble. From a man with fifty years of experience in the bush you can gain a half century of woods wisdom—by a friendly and frank desire to learn. The dangerous traveler is the one with a little knowledge who doesn't seek advice.

KEEPING THE PACK LIGHT

HEAP BIG PACK LITTLE GRUB
INDIAN—HEAP BIG GRUB LITTLE PACK

As a final caution, I say: Select your companions carefully, work with them awhile before you go. Learn to give and take. Choose a leader, agreed upon by all, who will work for the benefit of all!

SELECTING YOUR ROUTE

The selection of your route takes care and research. Write to the local authorities of the country in which you plan to travel. For example, if you are going to Canada, write first to the Provincial Department of Lands and Forests of the province which you have chosen for your trip; it can usually supply you with scale maps giving a general idea of the country. Occasionally they have larger-scale geological sheets that are more detailed.

There are many excellent canoeing trips available which start from auto roads or rough tote roads; but I believe the remoter regions to be those lying off the route of the great railroads in Canada, beyond the terminus of the automobile highways. My own favorite region is that serviced by the following railroads: the Algoma Central and Hudson Bay Railroad, the Canadian Pacific, the Ontario Northland and the Canadian National Railways. To obtain information regarding this area, write to the offices of the railroads. They will not only provide you with maps, but also help you to assemble your outfit, select your canoe at a very reasonable rate, and find a reliable guide. Many chambers of commerce are helpful; however, some try to steer a man who desires a wilderness trip to a summer resort area rather than to the bush country, although many resorts can help you take a nice trip and are very helpful with equipment and guides. One can often obtain some good blueprint maps from the forest rangers, and occasionally guides will permit you to copy some of their own map sketches, but the latter are often inaccurate and very local.

A word of caution: Get professional advice as to the best routes, if possible from persons who have been over them and who are reliable. Once we suffered for three weeks on half rations or less through what we called "dirty country." It was to have been a ten-day trip, and was marked out in a Detroit office by men in armchairs who had never been in the wilderness, but they thought it was going to be easy because it was a short-looking trip on paper. They sent their sons into a grueling experience. Later they were amazed to find the route included muskegs, mosquitoes, tortuous streams, (twenty-eight beaver dams in two miles in one stretch), a let-down by ropes through canyons and rock for forty-five miles (this took five hard days), dangerous rapids and back-breaking portages sometimes carrying over ridges five to eight hundred feet high. If someone had broken a leg, sprained a back, or become seriously ill, we might have buried him on that trip. Never again for me. A broken canoe or two would have been just as fatal, because it was next to impossible to walk out of that country, as it is in most Canadian bush areas, with their rough topography, lakes, bogs and spruce swamps.

Another important thing about your route is that if you are taking a pleasure trip, don't attempt to go too far. Plan to travel a day or two, then lay in for a day. Don't set up a strict schedule—the unknown factors of weather, trails, portages, possible mishaps, unexpected good fishing or illness may slow you down. On the other hand, higher water than expected may permit you to shoot rapids and thus save several portages; or a favorable tail wind, or a good-natured ranger or Mounted Policeman going your way with an outboard motor, may hook on and give you a lift. Consequently you will gain time. Avoid the individual whose meticulous habits will not allow him to relax because he must pass by a certain point of land at a quarter of two, be at an expected campsite at five twenty-three—or have a fit. Leave him at home! You came on the trip to relax, to become a vagabond, to live with nature, to meet what comes with the philosophical mind that builds for woods wisdom.

One time, someone asked Joe Friday, Indian guide at Temagami, how far it was to a point north (forty miles north) of Lady Evelyn Lake. His reply was, "About fifteen pounds of grub for each man and anywhere from two days to a week's journey." When a pompous member of the party who was critical of Joe's broad estimate made known his indignation none too gently, the following ac-

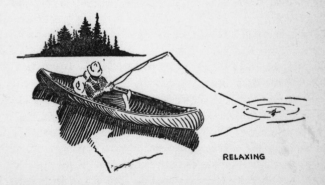

RELAXING

tion took place: Joe chewed his pipe, then after very sincere consideration he made this deeply religious reply, "I paddle and carry my canoe. The Lord watches over the weather. I tend to my business. He tends to His. If He sends a tail wind, two days, if He sends no wind, four days, and if He sends a head wind, one week. That is His business and guiding is mine. Don't try to tell either me or the Lord how to run our business."

Plan your voyage vagabond style so that you may "spade" water when you feel like it, or loaf along. You're out for fun, so why kill yourself? Know where you're going, have good maps and a good guide. Use skill, not "bull-strength." When you come to adversity, if the head wind is too strong, lay in for a day, repair equipment or do your washing. Relax, have fun, don't bite off more than you can chew.

SELECTING AND MAKING READY YOUR EQUIPMENT

From the time of the earliest inhabitants of the United States and Canada, contributions have been made by each country, and by others, to the development of modern wilderness traveling equipment. The intrepid French explorers, such as Etienne Brule and Jean Nicolet of the early seventeenth century, and later the Jesuit missionaries—Jacques Marquette, Jean de Brebeuf, Isaac Jogues and Charles Raymbault—who were among the first to venture into the Lake Superior and Lake Huron region, left accounts of their explorations, accounts which are full of the rugged beauty of the country and which often mention the suffering caused by their lack of proper clothing and equipment. Explorers, guides and the like learned to add many necessary articles to their equipment, from many sources.

From the early Indian comes the birchbark canoe; from the Eskimo and Indian, the sleeping bag; from the French, the bright woolen clothes; from the Swedes, the packsack; from the English, the wedge tent; from the Finn and the lumberjacks come the shoe-pack boots, wool socks, suspenders; and from the Americans, the rubber swampers and the slicker. Even the poncho from the tropics, via the British army, is a valuable piece of equipment. Supreme among all in travel efficiency (even beyond the high efficiency of horse travel) is the canvas-covered canoe, one of the most effective modes of transportation ever devised. There is a long history behind the development of the canoe and the paddle—these will be described in detail later. The canoe reached its highest perfection among primitive men in the birchbark model made by the Algonquins, who were living in Canada when the white man first came. All of the above-mentioned articles have been developed through more than three centuries by hundreds of experienced men over thousands of miles of wilderness trails.

In deciding what to wear, study the climatic conditions of the country into which you are going to be sure you really know what to expect. Let us plan, for instance, a trip into the Canadian bush. And because most people go to Canada in the summer, let us consider a summer outfit. It is, first of all, wrong to say that the North country is *cold* in the summer months (of course, fall, spring or winter trips are different). It is, usually, cool. Nevertheless, some of the most uncomfortable nights that I have experienced have been spent trying to sleep under wool blankets in June on the occasional hot, muggy nights when you have a choice of being roasted or eaten by mosquitoes—I can assure you that the former is always preferable. Be prepared mainly for cool weather from late June to the middle of September, and for some rain. You will find that two good blankets properly used or a light sleeping bag are enough. Take light warm clothes with a suit of lightweight underwear, 50 per cent wool, 50 per cent cotton. (Heavy wool underwear and heavy mackinaws are not necessary even in the Hudson Bay country.) Following is a list of what to wear from head to foot:

Old soft felt hat. Tropical helmets and hard hats get broken or blown by the wind. The idea of the hat is to keep the rain from running down your neck, the sun out of your eyes and the black flies out of your scalp. Preferably, the brim should be wide.

Light wool and cotton underwear, or shorts and T-shirts, or a set of both. Take at least two changes.

Soft wool shirt, buttoning clear down the front. You can open it and air-condition yourself, even to pulling out the tail. This protects you from cooling off too fast when perspiring, as wool is an excellent insulator.

Light, tough, full-length trousers with wide belt loops and well-sewed suspender buttons. (Dungarees are good.) *Caution:* No riding breeches, as these are not practical since they bind your legs when down on your knees paddling or carrying a heavy load, and you run the danger of pulling a muscle when circulation is cut off. Then when you pick up a load—Bingo!—and you are carried out on a stretcher.

Soft, thick wool socks. These are springy, giving good insulation against heat and are air-conditioned, letting the air circulate as you walk. Avoid cotton socks as they become sticky and cause sore feet and blisters.

Ankle-high to 10-inch leather boots. These should be laced boots with composition soles that will stick to rocks and give a sure footing. Leather soles get slippery, and hobnailed boots are fast passing from the picture. Swampers with rubber bottoms and leather tops are good in May, early June, September, October, and November, as they keep the feet dry in slush snow and yet do not cause excessive perspiration as do all rubber-laced boots that come up over the calf of the leg. The latter cut off circulation while one is paddling and leg injury may result. A boot height of ten inches is enough to brace ankles and protect them from the brush and rocks.

A wide, soft leather belt to be worn loosely. This type of belt is necessary for the same reason that you wear suspenders—so that belly muscles will work while you paddle and not rest against the belt; consequently, when you get out of the canoe for a portage, no muscles will be pulled as you roll up a hundred-pound canoe on your shoulders.

Wide elastic suspenders with leather fasteners. These hold up your pants. Simple, isn't it? but very comfortable. Did you ever try to carry a heavy load with your pants coming down? Suspenders prevent this embarrassment, especially when you are trying to show the ladies on the trip what a "he-man" you are. It may be unromantic, but it is sensible, to wear them; and on the other hand, you can't afford to overlook the fact that a wide belt suggested above helps to hide that over-development of the belt line from last winter which you hope to remove.

A neckerchief or bandana. This is practical to break the wind on cold days; to keep flies and mosquitoes off your neck; to wear on your head at night when it is cold, etc.

A shower-proof windbreaker, preferably wool-lined, to slip on in
evenings and on cool days, and to use as a knee-pad while paddling.

This wearing outfit should be well broken in before you start,
to make sure that it is comfortable. Extras to take are: poncho
or slicker (poncho is better as it covers the knees if you have to
paddle in the rain; extra pairs of socks, an extra pair of underwear, a heavy-duty cotton shirt for warm days; on long trips, an
extra pair of light trousers, handkerchiefs, and a light-weight slip-
over sweater for the colder days at the end of the summer; pair of
light buckskin gloves for sore hands, and a light pair of moccasins
or tennis shoes for around camp. Pajamas are considered necessary
by the more civilized. Swimming suits are carried in mixed (male
and female) groups.

For the ladies, the same type of outfit is best. Skirts aren't too
practical as mosquitoes and black flies have absolutely no sense of
decorum. Need I say more? The first day always ends with women
borrowing the men's extra pants in which to finish the trip. It's
always a struggle between modesty and a healthy desire to take a
full swing at the unabashed intruders. The bugs always win, and
you'll find that the ladies usually retreat into a pair of full-length
pants that can be stuffed into boots.

YOUR TRAIL EQUIPMENT

The Canoe. A sixteen-foot canoe is the usual traveling equipment. The Peterboro, Chestnut, or Old Town canvas-covered
canoe—with at least a thirty-four inch center width, twelve-to
thirteen-inch depth at the middle; shoe-keeled; low-prowed with a
slight lift at the bow and stern and flat-bottomed—is the best all-
round canoe. For heavy loads in open lakes or heavy white-water
rapids, I prefer the same type—but seventeen feet in length. Choose
your canoe for strength, good repair; it should be as light as possible. The average weight of the sixteen-foot canoe when dry is from
seventy to eighty-five pounds. The seventeen-foot will run ten to
fifteen pounds heavier. I have found all-metal canoes to be rather
rigid, stiff and noisy, and they pound in waves, but these are in use
more and more every year. The all-wood Peterboros are perhaps
the nicest handling canoes, but easily broken and have a tendency to

warp, water-log and develop open seams if laid in the sun. The plywood canoes are not yet too well known, and the birchbarks are becoming scarcer each year. The birchbarks are the next best canoe to the canvas-covered canoe, but they take constant care since they water-log rather easily.

The Paddles. Take one extra for each canoe and keep it handy in case of any emergency. The paddle blade should be well balanced to the handle or shaft and should not be too narrow or too wide. Maple is the best wood if it is thin enough so as not to be too heavy. It gives a nice spring not only when you are paddling but also when you are carrying the canoe on your shoulders. Spruce and ash are also good woods for paddles, but they fray out at the ends and are stiff, having little spring when paddling. As to length, the bow or front paddle requires a shorter blade which, when stood on end, should come to about a person's chin when he is standing erect. The stern paddle comes to the eyes or the top of the head. Be sure that they are in good shape, either well varnished or well oiled.

The Packsack. Two types are in general use in Canada. *First,* the Hudson Bay rucksack, which has leather shoulder straps, tump line and cross-tie straps from the front top, and buckles in the back about halfway up on each side with a "tuck over" top as shown in the sketch. *Second,* the Duluth pack, which is similar, but which has no cross straps; it does have a flap that comes halfway down the back, and three adjustable tie-buckle straps on the end of the flap, and it buckles in three places in the center of the back. These two types come in various sizes, the average being twenty inches high, twenty inches wide and eight to ten inches in depth. Be sure that the packs you choose are of strong canvas with taped reinforced seams, and water-proofed; the straps must be reinforced with a leather patch inside and out, being both riveted and sewed. The packs described above are comfortable, low riding (on the hips), with the strap attachments forward and center at the top so they will ride between the shoulder blades and the bottom of the shoulder straps with an adjustable buckle at the lower inside corners. For extra food and equipment for long trips, often light, strong, canvas-covered wooden wanigan boxes with tump lines and rounded corners are good. A newer box that is appearing in the North country is a telescope, fiberboard box with a tump line.

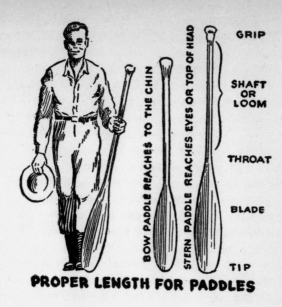

BOW PADDLE REACHES TO THE CHIN

STERN PADDLE REACHES EYES OR TOP OF HEAD

GRIP

SHAFT OR LOOM

THROAT

BLADE

TIP

PROPER LENGTH FOR PADDLES

TYPE OF PADDLES

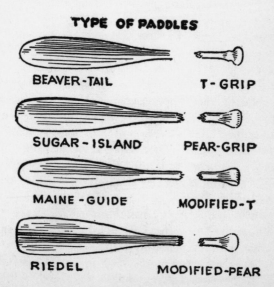

BEAVER-TAIL

T-GRIP

SUGAR-ISLAND

PEAR-GRIP

MAINE-GUIDE

MODIFIED-T

RIEDEL

MODIFIED-PEAR

This is proving to be excellent equipment, since it is light, strong and flexible enough to stand the terrific beating that all pack equipment takes along the trail. Pack boxes should not be more than thirty inches high, twenty inches wide and fourteen inches deep so that they will fit snugly in a canoe and on your back. Pack frames are frequently found in the Northwest, and the canvas-covered Adirondack pack basket is used by many.

The Tent. For years I used a trail tarpaulin tent that weighed only four or five pounds, but now I prefer an insect-proof tent such as the explorer tent or the wedge tent. My own choice is the wedge tent, with tabs about three-fourths of the way up so that it can be tied out (giving more headroom) by running a rope to a limb of a tree and pulling the sides outward. A wedge tent for four, with a sewed-floor and marquisette-mesh door covering to guard against insects, is the ideal canoe tent. When dry, it weighs from ten to twelve pounds (Egyptian silk) and can be rolled into a small bundle and carried in a pack. It sheds rain because of the steep pitch of its roof, stands up in a heavy wind, and is roomy and comfortable. Don't take tent pegs. There are a million within sight unless you are up on the tundra land. Once I saw an Englishman with three guides straining and carrying a heavy tent with iron tent pegs and collapsible ridge poles. A word of caution about your tent: Be sure that it is waterproof as well as spark-proof and mildew-proof before you leave on a trip. Do not roll it wet or it will mildew if it has not been treated.

Sleeping Equipment. A light, duck-feather sleeping bag with a hood, put out by the Supply Department of the Boy Scouts of America, is ideal for bush trips. Sleeping bags of down are also excellent equipment. Both types roll into a small ball weighing only two or three pounds. Two heavy army blankets and a good ground cloth or poncho made into the envelope style of bed are good equipment. Horse-blanket pins are handy for pinning up blankets and can be carried. If it gets too chilly at night, sleep in your long underwear and pajamas. Most people carry too much sleeping equipment. One time a French-Indian guide and I slept for three weeks with only an army blanket with a hole burned in it and a half pup tent between the two of us. We slept under a propped-up canoe with balsam boughs over and under us, and used a reflector fire, for there was frost every night.

Axe, Knife, Sharpening Stone and File.   There should be one axe per canoe. The single-bitted "three-quarter" axe is probably the best. It has a two- or three-pound head, according to the axe, with a twenty-eight-inch handle. It should be muzzled at all times except when being used and should always be kept sharp with an axe file, which all woodsmen carry, and the edge finished with an oil stone that is also an indispensable part of your equipment.

Your knife, if a belt-knife, should be strong, thin-bladed with a rounded point and not over five or six inches in length. It should be kept in a deep case-sheath carried far back on the hip pocket and not over the groin where, in case of a fall, it might sever an artery.

A good jackknife is just as useful as a sheath knife and is much easier to carry. I have an old jackknife that has skinned bear, deer and fish, and it only has a four-inch blade. Avoid big, thick knives. They are used only by tenderfeet and small boys. Another necessary piece of cutting equipment for long trips is the efficient "Swedish saw," which is flexible and can be rolled into a small bundle. A whip-saw can quickly be made from it by attaching a tree limb to the blade by a nail at each end. The bush knife or machete is becoming quite popular. Both it and the Swedish saw are very efficient for cutting brush, balsam and small trees.

Following are the contents of the carryall that should be found in most packsacks: toilet articles, a few nails, notebook and pencil, pliers, a roll of wire, needle and thread, buttons, some linen thread and beeswax, a sewing awl for leather, a couple of candles and some paraffined (waterproofed) matches. The carryall, or "ditty bag," as it is often called, is usually a small canvas bag with tie strings. Every woods traveler should have one.

Map Case.   It is always well to have a small oilskin map case which can also enclose your notebooks and writing material.

First-Aid Kit.   A standard auto first-aid kit—plus such extras as sulfa pills, sulfa powder for wounds, a box of good cathartic pills, aspirin, halozone tablets for water purification (should there ever be a question of its purity), a temperature thermometer, tweezers, scissors, and a pair of close-cut pliers for removing fish-hooks—is necessary. If on a long trip far from civilization, you will also need a suture and sewing kit. Also carry a bottle of olive oil with which to rub hands and face each day. This gets them into good condition, preventing blisters on the hands and windburn and sunburn on the face. It might be good to have your doctor, as well as a trained first-aid man, check and approve your supplies.

Canoe-Repair Kit. This is essential and should contain marine canoe glue, canvas for patching, a few brass tacks and nails; a small roll of light, strong copper wire; a canvas needle, twine, pliers and scissors.

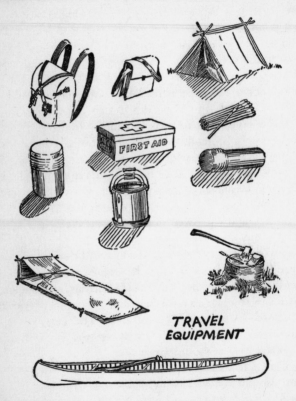

TRAVEL
EQUIPMENT

Cooking and Eating Kit. This should nest and fit together to make as small a bundle as possible, thus eliminating any rattle when carried and enabling you therefore to see more wildlife and game. (See list of journey equipment for details.) A package of paper towels is a good modern addition to the kitchen kit. A number of canvas sacks of varying sizes with tie strings should be made to carry your food. Sugar sacks or salt sacks will do nicely.

Other Necessary Items. These are compass and maps, and rope (there should be an average of fifty feet in length of quarter-inch manila or heavier cotton line for each canoe).

Fishing Tackle. There will be a chapter in detail on this later.

Hunting Equipment. This should be carried in hunting season only and with proper permits. More about this later.

Camera and Fragile Perishable Equipment. Such articles should be in tight, moisture-proof cases made of rubberized canvas, oilskin or metal. Films are best kept in screw-top or compression-topped cans. Once I worked for a newsreel company for several weeks filming big game, and all of their film, except when in the camera, was kept in air-tight metal containers. Airplanes would fly the "takes" out every few days.

Below is a list of equipment which has proved satisfactory and will serve as a good check list for you.

Personal and Party Journey Equipment for a Party of 4 Canoes and 8 People

NECESSARY CLOTHES FOR EACH PERSON	NECESSARY PERSONAL EQUIPMENT
Felt hat with wide brim	Pack (large)
Neckerchief	Hand axe
Shirt of strong material	Knife (scout or hunting knife)
Trousers of strong material: e.g., dungarees	Ground cloth
Heavy wool socks	2 heavy wool blankets or sleeping bag
Heavy leather shoes, at least ankle high, and with composition soles	Toilet kit:
Underwear	1 towel, soap, comb, toothbrush and paste, talcum, mirror, razor, extra razor blades, brush
Handkerchiefs	Notebook and pencil
Wide leather belt	Match case or paraffined matches (in pliofilm moistureproof bag)
Suspenders	Camera and films
	Olive oil for hands and face

Personal small first-aid kit: with any medicine or pills added that you may need, such as aspirin, cathartics, etc. (put pills in sealed moistureproof cellophane or plio-film.)

Personal emergency kit (small) with compass, map, concentrated food, whistle, extra paraffined matches, salt (waterproofed), fishhooks, and line

Bug-dope (repellent)

EXTRA CLOTHES FOR EACH PERSON

Pair of tennis shoes or moccasins
2 pairs of extra underwear
1 extra pair heavy wool socks
1 extra pair light wool socks
4 handkerchiefs
Poncho or slicker
Extra pair light pants for long trips

DESIRABLE EQUIPMENT TO HAVE

25-foot rope
Compass
Flashlight
Sharpening stone
Axe file
Camera
Sewing kit
Binoculars
Fishing tackle
Candles
Fly dope
Neat's foot oil for leather

JOURNEY EQUIPMENT FOR ENTIRE PARTY

1 large wedge tent and fly
Maps and compass
1 tarpaulin tent (trail tent)
4 16-foot canoes, 10 paddles
200 feet of rope and twine
300 feet of copper wire
One ¾ axe and file per canoe
1 large first-aid kit and medical supplies
1 canoe repair kit:
  marine glue, canvas patches, few brass tacks and nails, canvas needle, twine, pliers, scissors
Mosquito canopies, 1 Flit (DDT) and Flit Gun
Cooking and eating kit
Nest of pails—3 gal., 2 gal., 1 gal., ½ gal., 2 12-inch steel skillets with folding handles, 4-qt. tea and coffee pot; qt. grease can with screw top

JOURNEY EQUIPMENT FOR ENTIRE
PARTY

8 plates
8 cups (granite ware)
8 knives, forks, spoons
2 large serving spoons
1 pancake turner
1 kitchen knife
laundry soap
5 dish towels
1 box Brillo
Canvas bag with straps in which
    to nest cook kit.

As a final word on what to take, remember—*Take only what you need.* And cut down on weight and bulk of equipment so you can carry the most important item—*food!* Don't forget what John Wabsquaw said, "Indian—heap big grub, little pack." Leave your extras at home. You can't eat them, and you won't have to pack them on your back.

PLANNING AND PACKING FOOD AND COOKING GEAR

One time I met a party right up in the bush so that I didn't have time to get to the railroad tracks to check their outfit and "chuck" before they started. Never again! We cached 150 pounds

THE INDISPENSABLES

of extra stuff in a tree, including iron tent pegs. We planned a circle trip and ate up like fury four cases of canned goods (before we got up into the big lakes where we would encounter heavy seas and some long portages) so as not to break our backs on the portages with the load that they had brought. Much to my chagrin, I discovered they had forgotten to bring along three indispensable items—matches, axe, and salt. I had just finished a long trip so we made twelve paraffined matches do for six days until we could detour forty miles out of our way. During this time we ran into some bad head winds before we reached the Hudson Bay Post where the factor sold us the much-needed articles. Always have your guide check over your outfit and grub before you go.

Suppose we take a look first at planning your menu. The important thing is to remember that you cannot judge your menu and the amount of food you will need by the way you eat back home. You will eat twice as much or more after a few days on the trail, and your guide and woodsmen companions are used to eating heavily at all times. It takes coal in the boiler to drive a two-hundred pound man with 125 pounds on his back over a rough portage or with the equivalent in front of his paddle when he is underway. The major factor to happiness on the trail is plenty of well-cooked high calorie food. I once had two bankers argue that they didn't use much sugar. They refused to listen to advice, but I secretly took a ten-pound sack of sugar in my pack. To their utter amazement they had eaten up their supposed two weeks' supply in just four days, and had I been of the character of one of them, I could have sold my ten pounds of sugar for fifty dollars a pound within a week. The body craves fuel, and sugar is one of nature's best.

A word of caution about taking concentrated foods. We used to call them "constipated foods," for they will do just that. They are good for emergency rations and good as a fill-in, but who wants to live on powdered soup for two weeks? On the other hand, since World War II there have been developed many fine dehydrated vegetables and fruits that can be used, such as shredded potatoes, spinach, beets, carrots, onions, cabbage, peaches, apricots, apples, and many others. The use of these will save you fifty percent of the weight of your food, but remember that they must be kept dry and, if possible, in air-tight containers as they all absorb moisture and can easily be rendered useless.

Powdered milk can be bought from your local baker, and you should get the powdered whole milk if at all possible. Many people do not like powdered milk because they don't know how to use it. It must first be placed in a pan or bucket and enough cold water added slowly and mixed with a spoon until the milk is uniform paste with no lumps. Continue to add cold water slowly until it is of the right consistency. Then here is the trick—add a pinch of salt to the pint and a spoonful of sugar, place it in a tightly covered bucket, and shake vigorously for a few minutes. Remove the lid, pour back and forth from one bucket to another as the air works into the liquid and helps to produce a fine-tasting milk. In making cocoa, the same general method is applied—mix the cocoa, sugar and milk dry; add cold water to make the paste and boiling water to finish the drink. Powdered milk is undoubtedly one of the finest additions to wilderness diet.

BALANCED RATIONS

Suppose we take a look at some of the "natural" concentrated foods—flour, corn meal, cheese, butter, rice, dried beans, chipped beef, bouillon cubes, bacon, raisins, prunes, dried apricots and peaches. These all give a maximum of food value with a small moisture content and can be carried in light pliable containers such as canvas bags that will nest down smoothly into a pack sack. I am a firm believer, however, that certain heavier, moisture-containing foods are indispensable to keeping one from being "stalled" or, in other words, losing one's appetite, and these are a few small heads of cabbage and a few lemons. One soon gets to craving green stuff that the dried varieties don't seem to satisfy. Anyone who has been in the woods, in the army, or aboard ship soon realizes the need for fresh fruit, the most satisfying of which is lemons. The British Army the world over is known as consisting of "limeys" because of their habit of carrying lime juice. They learned through hard experience the advantage of having it as part of their regular rations. Following are five rules that should be followed in planning your menu:

Avoid canned goods! Plan it so that you can use such light foods as the dehydrated or the natural concentrated ones.

Plan a balanced dried diet, including meat, vegetables (one green vegetable a day), cereal, fruit, beverages and condiments. Take some candy along. It helps.

Select food that can be packed in cloth bags and avoid those foods with sharp corners. This will save space in packing, and those sharp corners will not dig through a packsack into your back.

Plan a menu that is simple, appetizing, and one that may be quickly and easily cooked. You're out for fun and cooking can be great fun, but you don't want to spend too much time doing it.

Take one extra day's rations per week per person. This is a safeguard if you have a delay in getting out of the bush or if you care to invite a fellow traveler whom you meet on the trail to have supper with your gang. Better to have a little extra than not enough!

Now to the actual planning and packing of the food. We have in the past arrived on a late train (9:30 P.M.) from the bush, and after the usual goodbyes to the party leaving, met the new party, planned their menu and bought enough food and supplies for eight men for twenty days. Eight o'clock the next morning found us aboard the train heading for the wilderness. We had also checked all their personal equipment, fishing tackle, cameras, film and still managed to get a few hours of sleep before we left. This requires efficient organization and accurate knowledge based on past experience. For a twenty-day trip, I have found it a good practice to repeat the menu every five days. It helps to simplify the supply list planning and purchasing and is spaced far enough apart so as not to become monotonous.

There are four steps to getting the grub on the trail: planning the menu; preparing the quantity check and cost list; packing; and shipping. Let's take each in order.

Planning the Menu.   First, a menu. The sample given below is a seven-day menu. You will note that the fruit dish for supper is made in quantity to cover the amount needed for breakfast. This is a definite time-saver. When the bread runs out, enough bannock is made at breakfast to carry over for lunch. Packing a lunch in a separate sack each morning will save you time at noon. (Note: Bread can be carried for about the first three days. Using a minimum of fried foods is a good health practice.)

| CAMP | TRAIL | CAMP |
BREAKFAST	LUNCH	DINNER
1st Prunes and lemon *day* Scrambled eggs Bacon Toast Coffee	(Packed each morning in one bag) Bread, butter and jam Cocoa Summer sausage Raisins Candy bar	Creamed chipped beef on toast Mashed potatoes Stewed corn Bread and butter Tea Stewed apricots
2nd Stewed apricots *day* Pancakes Smoked sausage Coffee	(At this point it is good fishing) Boiled trout Potatoes Bread and butter Raisins Tea Candy bar	Spaghetti dinner Slaw Bread and butter Cocoa Apple sauce
3rd Apple sauce *day* French toast Syrup Bacon Coffee	Jam and peanut butter sandwiches Chipped beef (eaten dry) Cocoa Fig newtons Candy bar	Boiled ham and cabbage Potatoes Carrots Bread and butter Tea Peach turn-overs
4th Stewed peaches *day* Fried mush and syrup Smoked sausage Coffee	Pea soup Bannock and jam Cheese Tea Dried apricots Candy bar	Baked beans (dried) with bacon and syrup Spinach Bannock and butter Cocoa Apple sauce with cinnamon
5th Apple sauce *day* Creamed ham on biscuits Biscuits and butter	Biscuit and ham sandwiches Biscuits and jam Cocoa Raisins	(good fishing here) *Fish supper* Boiled fillet of wall-eyed pike Potatoes

CAMP	TRAIL	CAMP
BREAKFAST	**LUNCH**	**DINNER**

Coffee
(Fix extra biscuits
  and ham for
  lunch)
	Candy bar	Carrots and peas
		Slaw
		Prunes and lemon
		Bannock
		Tea

6th Prunes and lemon
day Bacon, scrambled
  eggs (dry)
Bannock (coffee-
  cake style, add-
  ing milk, sugar,
  cinnamon)
Coffee
Make Bannock
  for lunch
	Bannock and jam
	Cheese
	Tea
	Dry peaches
	Candy bar
		(Blueberries here)
		Creamed chipped beef
		  on bannock
		Mashed potatoes
		Spinach
		Bannock and butter
		Cocoa
		Blueberry cobbler

7th Fresh blueberries
day with milk
Pancakes and
  syrup
Bacon
Coffee
	Bannock and fresh
	  blueberry jam
	Chipped beef (dried)
	Raisins
	Candy bar
		Ham
		Potatoes
		Escalloped corn
		Bannock and tea
		Apple turnovers

Preparing the Quantity Check and Cost List. The second step is the checking of the menu against the quantity and buying list. Make for yourself a mimeographed form as shown below, dividing your food into its five main divisions. One man then calls the menu. When he calls "coffee," for instance, make a check-mark by coffee, cream and sugar. When bannock is called, check flour, short-ening, salt, baking powder, except that it is not necessary to check salt each time as plenty will be taken anyway. Not so for sugar. Check it each time as a larger poundage will be used. Below is the check list for the menu given above. Try it. Have one read the menu and another check off the items as they are called.

Note: Prices given vary a great deal and are therefore not ac-curate—weights used are:

Ration: 1 person, 1 meal.

Quantity: Number of persons x number of meals x ration equals pounds.

Cost: Cost per pound or per item.

Trip to Hilda—Michipicoten Harbor
No. days (date) from 8-1 to 8-8
No. persons   8

MEAT

	MEALS #	RATION #	QUANTITY	UNIT COST	TOTAL
Bacon IIIIII	6	.20	9.6#	.37	3.55
Ham IIII	4	.40	12.8#	.40	5.12
Summer sausage III	3	.30	7.2#	.28	2.02
Chipped beef IIII	4	.10	3.2#	.85	3.72
Canned butter IIIIIIIIIII	11	.05	5.0#	.52	2.60
Dry eggs III	3	.10	2.4#	.50	1.20
Cheese II	2	.24	3.9#	.45	1.76
Crisco IIIIIIIIIII	11	.05	4.4#	.20	.88
Dry milk IIIIIIIIIIIIIII	15	.04	4.8#	.20	.96
Peanut butter I	1	.20	1# jar	.40	.40
			54.3#		22.21

CEREALS

	MEALS #	RATION #	QUANTITY	UNIT COST	TOTAL
Bread IIIIIIIII	9	.20	10.4 (1 vs)	.12	1.30
Cookies I	1	.30	2.4#	.25	.60
Flour IIIIIIIIIIIIII	14	.15	16.8#	.10	1.68
Pancake flour II	2	.20	3.0#	.25	.75
Corn meal I	1	.15	1.2#	.10	.12
Oatmeal (carry as extra ration for emergency)	1			.20	.20
Spaghetti I	1	.30	3 bxs	.40	1.20
			36.6		5.85

VEGETABLES

	MEALS #	RATION #	QUANTITY	UNIT COST	TOTAL
Dry spuds IIIII	5	.15	6	.20	1.20
Dry Corn III	3	.15	3.6	.30	1.08
Fresh cabbage III	3	.25	6	.05	.30
Carrots, dry III	3	.15	3.6	.30	1.08
Peas, dry I	1	.15	1.0	.40	.40
Pea soup I	1	.15	1.0	.40	.40
Dry baked beans I	1	.20	2.0	.18	.36
Spinach, dry II	2	.15	2.4	.40	.96
			25.6		5.78

FRUITS

	MEALS #	RATION #	QUANTITY	UNIT COST	TOTAL
Prunes III	3	.18	4.4	.20	.88
Dry peaches III	3	.15	3.6	.25	.90
Dry apricots IIII	4	.15	4.8	.25	1.20
Dry apples IIIII	5	.08	3.2	.50	1.60
Raisins IIIII	5	.15	6.0	.30	1.80
Lemons III	3	1 doz.	3.0	.50	1.50
Jam IIIIII	6	1 qt.	2.0	.40	.80
			27.0		8.68

CONDIMENTS AND BEVERAGES

	MEALS #	RATION #	QUANTITY	UNIT COST	TOTAL
Baking Powder IIIIIIIIII	10	.01	1.0	.30	.30
Sugar IIIII IIIII IIIII					
IIIII IIIII IIIII IIIII	35	.05	14.0	.07	.98
Brown sugar IIII	4	.05	1.6	.10	.16
Tea IIIIIIII	8	.01	.5	1.00	.50
Coffee IIIIIIII	8	.03	1.5	.40	.60
Cocoa IIIIII	6	.03	1.5	.50	.75
Salt 212			2 lbs.	.10	.20
Pepper 21			2 oz.		.25
Cinnamon 5			1 oz.		.30
Vinegar			1 pt.	.20	.20
			23.3 lbs.		4.24

EXTRAS

	MEALS #	RATION #	QUANTITY	UNIT COST	TOTAL
Candy bar	7	.2	11.2	.05	.56
Laundry soap	2 brs.	1.0	2.0	.10	.20
Brillo		1 bx	.5	.25	.25
Paper towels		2 bdls.	2.0	.15	.30
Matches		2 bxs	.5	.05	.10
			16.2		1.41

TOTAL CALCULATION	POUNDS	COST
Meats	54.3	$22.21
Cereals	36.8	5.85
Vegetables	25.6	5.78
Fruits	22.0	8.68
Condiments, Drinks	23.3	4.24
Extras	16.2	1.41
	183.2	$48.17

TOTAL

8 persons in party, including the guide:

Total pounds: 183.2 ÷ 8, equals 22.9 pounds of food for each to carry.

Average cost: $48.17 ÷ 7, equals $6.88 each. (Guide's food is furnished; rest of party pay for it.)

Average cost per meal: $48.17 ÷ 21 meals, equals $2.29 as cost per meal for 8.

Average cost per person per meal: $48.17 ÷ 168 meals (21 × 8), equals 28.6¢.

Note that cost will vary with rise and fall in prices.

Packing. The grub is all placed in individual cloth bags, and the item name is written with black crayon on the outside so that it can be identified without opening, such as tea, coffee, bacon, ham, and prunes. We have on the above list approximately forty-four items, about thirty-eight of which need to go in canvas bags. After all are in the bags, then divide them up evenly as to bulk and as to weight. A shipping tag is then issued to each man, and

in black crayon pencil or India ink he writes the list of items as-
signed to his packsack, and the tag is tied with heavy cord on the
outside. *Now*, on the trail anyone can tell what food is in whose
pack by just looking at the tag. This makes for good economy in

CANVAS BAGS···
SAVE WEIGHT, PACK EASILY

time and temper when one is trying to find things when the gang
is out fishing. It also necessitates only a minimum of digging into
someone else's packsack, this being good human relations on the
trail. The food is then stowed away in each packsack with the least
perishable and the heaviest at the bottom and so on up. The blankets and clothes are placed against the front of the packsack or, in
other words, the part that is against your back, to make carrying as
comfortable as possible. Cameras, film, first-aid kit, ditty bag, notebooks and maps are placed on top so that they are readily accessi-
ble. You are now ready to close up the pack, fasten the straps down
snug, and are almost ready to go. (Note: The guide usually carries the sugar, flour and bacon as a safeguard since these are the
basic staples.)

TIE FISHING RODS
INSIDE THE GUNNELS

KEEP CANOE REPAIR
KIT AND 50 FEET OF
ROPE READY FOR
USE···STOW IN BOW

PREPARING THE CANOE

Shipping. Finally we are ready to have the canoes, with the
supplies, shipped. First, tie the paddles in securely. If you have a
fishing rod, tie it up inside under the gunwales. Be sure that
each canoe has a 50-foot hank of rope tied securely and jammed

into the bow under the wedge. Some campers tie a small canoe
repair kit up under the wedge inside the stern of each canoe. With
this preparation completed, you are ready to hit the long trail. So
load the canoes on the cars or onto the train platform. Each man
brings up his own pack. A final check is then made of everyone
and everything, and at last you are ready to go. You have everything that you need, nothing that you do not need; you are ready
for action and you have taken every possible preparation and pre-
caution. And if, in addition, you have selected a good guide, you
will have an unforgettable experience. Let us go back now and
consider the guide.

SELECTING YOUR GUIDE

Take great care in selecting your guide, especially if the trip
you are planning is your first. Write long in advance to the local
authorities in the town that will serve as your final outfitting place
or your last port of call, so to speak. They will be glad to line
up a reliable guide for you.

Let's be very frank about this. French-Canadians, in spite of
occasional local political opinions, are usually the best guides for
all-around companions in the woods. They are usually intelligent,
picturesque, light-hearted, good entertainers, clean, and have a
deep love and understanding of the wilderness. They will provide
you with some unforgettable moments, especially during exciting incidents on the trail or in the evening around the fire, when
you will enjoy their pidgin English-French vernacular. English-
Canadians and Scotch-Canadians are usually more reticent but are
excellent canoemen and bushmen, as are the Swedes and Finns.
Eskimos are good companions but are not very skilled as cooks
and have a tendency to fry everything. As for the Indian as a
guide and companion, some of the best guides that I have known
have been Indians and also some of the worst. You will find a
wide variance among them. They are good quiet companions, and
if you win their confidence they have a depth of woods knowledge
that surpasses all others; but if you get a bad one who likes whiskey
too much, he can be a risky proposition, especially if he is of
"mixed-blood." Depend on your outfitter or your railroad traffic
manager to help you find a good one. Also remember that your

guide should know the country where you are going. First, a guide must be reliable and experienced and know the country. Second, he must be able to cook and handle a canoe. Other qualities to look for are cleanliness, congeniality and trustworthiness.

As to your attitude towards your guide: you pay his fee which averages about six dollars per day, and his expenses in such matters as meals, food, transportation, and journey equipment, except for his own personal effects. Many people make the mistake of considering him a servant. This is one of the shortcomings of new travelers in the bush. Your guide is your companion, adviser, your teacher and your protector in emergencies. Your life often depends on his knowledge, judgment, advice and skill. It is his job to show you the way, show you where the fish and game are, to see that you are fed and that you sleep well. But he expects you to do your complete share of the work and chores on the trail and in camp and to paddle your end of the canoe. Don't call him "mister"—call him by his first name at once, and he'll do the same. If you are humble, seeking his advice and knowledge, you will be able to draw a great deal of trail and woods lore from him. As mentioned before, let him check your complete outfit, let him help with the final supplies, and feed him all he can eat (which is twice as much as you'll eat) and you will have a wonderful time.

One of the first things to do after getting acquainted is to check the route with your guide. Help him to get the best maps that you can find and then go to the nearest Forest Ranger Station and have the maps checked by them with the guide. Often they will give you advice on short cuts, thus avoiding bad country which sometimes is impossible to detect on a map. They will tell you where different kinds of fish and good campsites are located. For safety's sake let the authorities of the railroad and the Forest Rangers know your expected route, where you will be approximately each day, and when you will be out. This is for your own safety, for if an emergency should arise, such as serious illness or death in your family, they can find you by plane or canoe or both. Also, leave your home address with them in case there should be an emergency involving yourself or other members of your party. If you are in a forest preserve or a national park, be sure to get a travel permit and follow the regulations as to the cutting of timber and the care of fires.

PREPARING FOR EMERGENCIES

Your final preparations for emergencies must include the selection of your first-aid kit. I shall discuss wilderness first-aid later on. But as I have mentioned before, be sure to take along a combination small but adequate first-aid kit and medical kit that has been checked by your doctor. The standard auto kit is good—Johnson & Johnson or Bauer & Black, or others. The kits mentioned are in canvas-covered metal boxes and contain the right supplies. To each kit should be added such medical supplies as a box of cathartics, boric acid, aspirin, spirits of ammonia, an extra tube of burn lotion or salve, Mentholatum, sulfa pills and powder from your doctor's prescription, a body thermometer, a small pair of scissors, tweezers and a strong pair of short-cut pliers to cut fishhooks out of the flesh. While we are on the subject of first-aid, let us look at the prevention side. Here are some things to watch out for:

SUNBURN

Sunburn. Keep your shirt on at all times. It's nice to have a coat of tan, but you can't carry a load on sunburned and blistered shoulders and back. Don't try to tell your guide that you don't sunburn. Even Indians do under the right conditions. Remember that on the water you get double reflection. Carry a bottle of olive oil and rub your hands, face and exposed parts a couple of times each day. It will not only keep your skin in good condition but also your lips from cracking and your hands from blistering. After several weeks of this your skin gets like fine tanned leather.

Your Eyes. If your eyes are sensitive to light, be sure to wear a pair of good dark glasses, at least for the first few days until your eyes get adjusted. You have only one pair of eyes—be cautious and save them all you can.

Insects. Here are mentioned the biting insects of the North country. Their "nuisance" qualities are, however, sometimes over-emphasized, but it's best to come prepared for the worst.

Mosquitoes (From early June to late August, diminishing toward the end of the summer). There are several varieties but no dangerous ones, such as the malaria mosquito. They poke holes in you, drink your blood if you let them, but it is possible to foil them if you understand their habits. They do not like sunshine or wind, not even a breeze, and they don't like smoke. They are found in the greatest numbers among trees, bushes, and grass and in the least on bare rock and open timber. They seem to like sandy beaches, spruce swamps and grassy places the best. Take an insect-proof tent or a mosquito-bar canopy. In recent years I have carried a can of Flit and a small spraygun to give my tent or mosquito-bar a good "going over" before I go to bed. Mix a little DDT (10 percent) with the Flit. It certainly helps and you'll gain hours of sleep. Mosquitoes attack usually at dawn, just after dark, and during the evening; on a rare "muggy" hot night they work all night long. If you don't have any Flit, smudge-pot them away by putting green leaves on the fire; or if "going light" with no tent, sleep close to the fire, and they will stay away. Remember, select your campsite on an island or a point, cut back the grass and brush, and let the breeze blow most of the mosquitoes away.

Black Flies (During June to the middle of July). The black fly is a character to be reckoned with. He looks like a very small housefly with a shiny black body. Unlike the mosquito, he works the "day shift." He appears mostly in burned or cut-over areas, or on dry hillsides, and will crawl and bite around sweaty tight places such as around your boot tops, belt, or under your arms and will also bite your scalp and crawl through your hair. He will swarm around your face and does not delicately puncture your skin as does the mosquito. He just bites out a chunk. The best protection from the black fly is to stay out of the bush in the middle of June, or if you are in the bush, to stay on the water or camp where the wind blows. Fly dope definitely helps. Kerosene helps around the tight spots. It is good to brush it on lightly with your fingertips. A stoic disregard will also help as the flies are a strain on your temper if you permit them to be. Head nets are effective, but when wearing one you have trouble using a tump line and carrying a canoe. Luckily for the North country, the fly season is short. Usually the last two or three weeks in June are the worst. But the catch is that at this time the big speckled trout takes the "dry fly" the best. So use your own judgment, brother. I still fight flies to get a big trout on a six-ounce fly rod.

Moose Flies They look like gray-bodied house flies. They hang around camp and crawl over you, occasionally taking a healthy bite. They seem to frequent clearings and old lumber camps. The best way to keep most of them away is to keep all food under cover and out of reach, keep garbage buried, and keep the camp clean.

Deer Flies These "buzz bombs" are not too common in the North country, but when you do get into them, they are vicious and bite as they alight. They are triangular in shape, with a large head, biting mandible, and black striped wings, and they frequent narrow alder-lined streams and portage trails. The best protection against them is to tie brush loosely around your head, face and neck so it will jiggle as you walk; however, this doesn't always work. Swatting is the best way.

Punks or "No See-Ems" These are tiny, almost invisible, midges that can filter through the smallest mesh. They are not common in the North country, but when you get them in the evening, they feel like hot sparks dropping on you. Smudges are effective; Flit is a definite cure.

A word to the wise: Don't let a few bugs stop you from going into the bush country. Just go prepared to combat them. Your sporting goods store will recommend several fly dopes, but remember that the pasty or salve types seem to stay effective longer. Go with an insect-proof tent and take a can of Flit. It's worth its weight. Also remember that the height of the insect season is usually late June and early July and tapers off so that the month of August finds only a small fraction of the insects that exist earlier in the summer. Most people do not know that the loveliest weather of the whole year in the North country is during the first few weeks in September. Usually one frost at least has settled the insect question. This is the time I like best—when the bugs are dead and the leaves begin to turn red and gold. So much for the bugs.

You are now ready to get under way. Your preparation is complete. Your grub is in the packsack. You have prepared for emergencies and checked your route. Your guide is squatting on his heels, talking to your partner, and he looks good. You have your canoes ready to ship. Your dress is comfortable and adequate. You have a good supply of tobacco and a bottle of tonic stowed among the blankets in your pack in case of need or the meeting of an old friend on the trail on a cool evening. The train will soon be in, and you're ready for high adventure. There's a tingling along your spine and a deep feeling of anticipation. You feel the age-old heart tug that calls you to far and distant places. Soon we'll get into the canoe and go paddling into the quiet country beyond the blue hills.

3

THE CANOE AND HOW TO USE IT

No boat or water craft has ever approached the canoe for efficiency in wilderness travel. There are various types of boats that are remarkably efficient in their particular locality and for their particular use, such as the kayak of the Eskimo, the pointer boat of the lumberjack, the bateau and York boats of the Hudson's Bay Company, the duck boat for local marsh hunting, the pirogue of the Louisiana swamps, the "Joe" boats of the entire Mississippi drainage, and many others. But nothing approaches the canoe for universal efficiency. World War II has brought us some new craft and improved mechanisms that have considerable use in wilderness travel—as the inflated rubber boat, the aluminum canoe and boat, improved outboard motor. Even improved amphibious planes are going to have real influence on travel in wild country.

A canoe, however, is a craft that anyone can learn to use efficiently in a comparatively short time with a little instruction, plus common sense, practice, and the observation of certain laws of balance and gravity. The thing to get clearly in mind, first of all, is that the canoe is one of the safest crafts afloat, for the popular conception that canoes upset inevitably is definitely false, childish and disgraceful. It is one of the most irritating notions that must always be overcome when teaching canoeing to a novice. It is absolutely unnecessary even to think of upsetting. There are thousands of people who throughout their lives travel thousands of miles in canoes and never upset. Most of these people can't even swim. The pseudo-tradition, therefore, that the canoe is an unsafe and hazardous craft is false. If one will learn and observe the basic fundamentals of handling it—namely, treat it with great care at all times, and keep one's weight low on the bottom and center and balance up the weight fore and aft—one can ride out wind, wave and white water that would swamp any other boat of equal displacement.

We shall take up the canoe and its use in seven sections described as follows:

> Where To Get Your Canoe Instruction
> Selecting Your Canoe and Its Parts
> Handling the Canoe on Land, Docking and Loading
> Fundamentals of Paddling a Canoe
> Canoe on Lake or Other Large Open Water
> Down-River Canoeing
> Up-River Canoeing

WHERE TO GET YOUR CANOE INSTRUCTION

There are many kinds of canoes and all have good and poor qualities, according to their design and the material used in their building. Your canoeing can be practiced in most of them quite satisfactorily. In fact, if you are planning a trip, a great deal of fun can be had by practicing for several weeks or months before you start, on some local stream, lake, park lagoon or pond, even in the local swimming pool. It must be remembered here that you cannot always depend upon your guide to teach you canoeing because he has been raised in a canoe and has learned to handle it with the ease that most children learn to ride a bicycle or to roller skate. Consequently, his reflexes are conditioned to a point where he can stand up, walk around and do other things in a canoe which are the result of a lifetime of practice, things which would be disastrous for the beginner to try and which he could probably never attain. Also many guides are poor teachers and cannot understand why people are so clumsy. They often do things automatically and do not always understand how they do it themselves. Just because a man is an Indian, Eskimo or a French Canuck is no sign that he is a good canoesman. Among the natives of a wilderness country, one finds a wide variance in canoeing ability. Until requirements for obtaining a guide's license in any given area are more definite, until rigid guiding requirements other than belonging to an association are established, one will not always be able to depend on the guide's ability to teach you how to get the most out of your canoe. In selecting your guide, it is best to investigate these qualities before you hire him. Good-quality guides, however, are often good instructors and a bush trip is more than just fun; it is an educational opportunity. If you show you are anxious to learn and you ask questions, your guide usually will respond gladly and teach you many things. Just watch him and you will learn a great deal. But above all, be humble; and when in doubt ask questions, but don't pester him.

A final word on preparing yourself for your trip. If you make use of the instructions in this book, you can teach yourself many things. Your local Boy Scout executive, water-front director, or the Red Cross boat and canoeing instructor will show you much about handling and paddling the canoe. You can practice for several weeks before starting. The joy of canoeing is that one is always learning new things about, and in connection with, it; and the years ahead of one can be rich in acquiring added knowledge about handling the canoe in various parts of the world, about meeting the local stream conditions whether one is on the Amazon, the Congo, the Niangua in the Ozarks of Missouri, or on the McKenzie or Peace River of the far North.

SELECTING YOUR CANOE AND ITS PARTS

Some information about choosing a canoe has been given in Chapter 2. Here I shall repeat part of the information in giving complete details as to the selection of your craft. The best all-around canoe for the average trip is a sixteen-foot "guide model" canoe (low ended) strongly and lightly built of cedar planking with strong, well-painted and -varnished canvas cover. For long trips or for rapids and white water, the seventeen-foot canoe is better although it is fifteen or twenty pounds heavier. There are many fine brands of canoes both in the United States and Canada,

two of the oldest and most famous being the Old Town of Maine
and the Peterboro of Peterboro, Ontario. Maybe you prefer an
aluminum canoe put out by Grumman or other companies, but the
fundamentals of selection are the same. First, the canoe should be
at least sixteen feet in length, twelve to fourteen inches in depth,
and at least thirty inches wide across the middle. It should not be
round or flat bottomed, but slightly curved. It should round up at
the sides to give maximum displacement in the water and the ends
should not taper off too quickly but be of adequate width and comfortable depth at the place where the paddlers rest. There should
be a lift of the keel, two or three inches at both ends, so that the
canoe can ride up on a wave or white water in rapids, rather than
plow through thus avoiding shipping of water. Also this rise is necessary in case one should hit a submerged log or rock by accident.
Your canoe must be made of the strongest yet lightest material,
and any brads, screws or other metal parts should be of brass, instead of steel or iron, to prevent rusting. This is especially true if
you are going to be in salt water. Select your canoe with care—
get the advice of your guide, if possible.

It is best for canoe travelers to know the names of the craft's
parts, many of them old in tradition. Thus, the left side of the
canoe is the port side and the right side is the starboard. The
railing or the side of a canoe that binds the ends of the ribs is in two
parts; the inside strip is called the in-wale and the outside one is
called the out-wale, and together they form the gunwale or gunnel.
This last-mentioned part runs the entire length of the canoe. The
front of a canoe is called the bow (sounds the same as "cow") and
the back end the stern. Supporting and holding apart the gunwales
are cross strips or braces known as spreaders or thwarts. The
strength of a canoe is made by bow-shaped pieces running from one
gunwale down across the bottom to the opposite gunwale. These
pieces, known as ribs, are in turn covered on the outside by thin
cedar boards known as planking. Covering the planking is canvas,
called sheeting by some. The canvas is stretched and shrunk tight
to the planking and soaked with linseed oil filled with white lead
and paint. Finally, it is covered with a coat of protective varnish
which reduces water soaking and friction when the canoe is in motion.

Around the outside of the bow and stern is a brass strip that is used for "fending-off" anything that might otherwise injure the canoe—it is known as the "bang strip." Along the bottom and running the full length of the canoe is a strip of hardwood that is known as the keel. There are two types of keels. One is the lake keel, about one-inch wide and tapered slightly up about one inch, which prevents side slipping in wind and open water like the center board of small sail craft. The other type of keel is the shoe keel, about two inches wide and about one-fourth to one-half inch thick, which allows side slipping but protects the bottom from rocks, logs or other abrasive materials. The latter keel is especially valuable for use on rivers where there is a possibility of rocks or logs and where side slipping is an important part of the guiding and steering. Perhaps the best all-around keel is the shoe keel.

PARTS OF THE CANOE

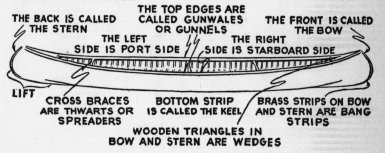

THE BACK IS CALLED THE STERN

THE TOP EDGES ARE CALLED GUNWALES OR GUNNELS

THE FRONT IS CALLED THE BOW

THE LEFT SIDE IS PORT SIDE

THE RIGHT SIDE IS STARBOARD SIDE

LIFT

CROSS BRACES ARE THWARTS OR SPREADERS

BOTTOM STRIP IS CALLED THE KEEL

BRASS STRIPS ON BOW AND STERN ARE BANG STRIPS

WOODEN TRIANGLES IN BOW AND STERN ARE WEDGES

One or two other parts of the canoe should be mentioned. The triangular blocks at the bow and stern of a canoe, where the gunwales come together, are called the wedges; and if they have been extended toward the paddlers, they are called decking. A recent innovation in the canoe has been the addition of the seat. And there is a question among many canoeists whether or not it is necessary, as the proper position for canoeing is down on one's knees resting back against the seat and not sitting on it.

I have described in the preceding paragraphs the fundamental parts of a canoe and mentioned the standard terms used in describing the various parts. However, there are sometimes local names for all these, and it is best not to correct a man employing local names, for who are we to tell him. He is right in his own locality and we should abide by it.

Selection of your paddles, too, has been previously mentioned in Chapter 2. The best are made of maple, but ash and spruce paddles also have good qualities. The blade should not be over six inches wide and not more than one-third the length of the paddle. A good smooth comfortable grip should be at the top and the shaft should be sturdy but not too thick. Look at the grain, especially on the shaft of the paddle, to be certain that it is true and not cross-grained. Look for breaks, cracks or checks in the wood; and sight along the shaft and blade to make sure the paddle is not warped or it won't ride true on your shoulder when you carry your canoe and it will have a tendency to twist in your hand when you stroke. You'll average about 25 to 30 strokes a minute, 450 strokes a mile,

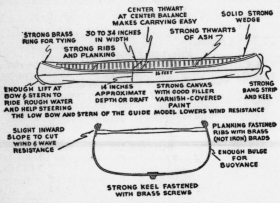

GOOD POINTS IN A CANOE

about 1,800 an hour when in steady motion and, in a good long day, between 15,000 and 18,000 strokes. A three-pound paddle carried forward or backward will be the equivalent of 54,000 foot pounds of work—about the same amount of energy that it takes a fireman to shovel coal for a 350-mile run on a steam passenger train. This is something to think about, and when one considers it in the light of 18,000 strokes, the "small matters" of weight, balance, trueness and even the varnish on the paddle become important factors. Select your paddle well. Let us repeat: the bow paddle stood on end comes up to the chin, while the stern paddle comes up to the eyes or top of the head. The stern paddle is longer since there is more need for length in steering, most of which is done from the stern position.

HANDLING THE CANOE ON LAND, DOCKING, AND LOADING

Let me describe the handling of the canoe on land, its docking and loading in about the way my old French-Canadian friend Phil Paquette would do it. Let us go along with him on a bush trip and see how he would acquaint new people with canoeing during the first few days. Let us listen to him closely while he explains some of the fundamentals of good canoemanship.

At the beginning of a trip, Phil Paquette explains the parts of the canoe and we select our paddles. Then comes the big moment —the launching of the canoes, the loading of the cargo, the getting aboard and starting. The guide demands absolute and concentrated attention as he drives home the point that 90 percent of all canoe damage is done on land and that one must be careful in handling canoes at all times, both on the land and in the water. This is a major responsibility of every individual. The measure of a good canoesman is in the absence of marks or scratches on his canoe, and in his ability to keep his shoes dry. In other words, the canoe is the woodsman's well-cared-for servant at all times and it in turn takes care of him.

There are several ways of picking up a canoe, Paquette points out to us, but perhaps the best way to do it alone is to stand in the center of the canoe and roll the canoe up sideways until the bottom is against your legs. Then your left hand grasps the near gunnel with your right hand. With a quick upward rolling motion the canoe can be rolled up on your back with the center thwart resting across your shoulders. This is good for short carries up to a quarter of a mile, after you are hardened up a bit. The same can be done by two men standing on the same side by the forward and back thwart and rolling the canoe up with the front and back thwarts resting on their shoulders. This makes a comfortable carry. To let the canoe down when carried singly, balance forward, bringing the front down. Then, with feet wide apart, shove your right hand up, holding your left hand steady and firm, twist to face the canoe as it gently rolls down on your legs and is eased to the ground. A little practice, the guide assures us, will teach us this valuable basic way of handling and carrying a canoe on land.

On your first day, however, we probably shall have a short carry of a few yards, with the guide's instructions, the two men in each group stand facing each other on opposite sides of the canoe at the center, which is resting bottom-down. Then, stooping down, they grasp the gunwales, lifting the canoe and carrying it forward simultaneously. The same can be done with two men standing at each end, reaching down, lifting and carrying the canoe by grasp-

TWO MAN

Lift and Carry

UP EDGE THE CANOE,
BOTTOM TOWARD YOU...
GRASP THWARTS WITH
RIGHT HANDS, GUNWALE
WITH LEFT HANDS

HEAVE WITH YOUR RIGHT HANDS
PUSH WITH LEFT·····TWIST
FORWARD AND ROLL THE CANOE
UP OVER YOUR HEADS

REMEMBER··IN CANOEING
IT'S TEAMWORK
THAT COUNTS

BALANCE UP, WATCH
YOUR FOOTING AND
YOU'RE OVER THE PORTAGE

ing under the bow and stern wedges or decking. The canoe then is eased into the water, bow forward, avoiding rocks and snags and is pulled up so that the stern rests gently on the side of the lake. We are now ready to load the canoe. In doing so, the sternman holds the end of the canoe firmly between his knees while the bowman piles the packs on the ground within reach of the sternman. Then, while the stern paddler holds the canoe steady, the bowman backs up into the canoe holding the gunwales to the center of the canoe and kneels down facing the sternman who is holding the canoe steady between his knees. Packs are then passed up to him by the sternman while he is holding the end of the canoe between his legs, thus freeing his hands to pass forward the duffle. The bowman packs it in snugly, being sure to distribute the weight evenly, center, fore and aft. If the waves seem high, or if there are rapids and white water to shoot, or if it looks like rain, poles are placed in the bottom of the canoe under the duffle to keep it out of any water that may come in. In cloudy weather, a tarpaulin or ground cloth, such as a half pup tent, is placed over the duffle and then a rope is tied back and forth across the canoe holding everything snugly.

DUFFLE TIED IN

While we are loading our canoe, so are the other members of the party—all under the guide's piercing scrutiny—and now his voice quietly instructs each man how to sit in a canoe. His instructions are something like this, "By Gar, thee tam has come for us to get started, but first nous allons avec le canoe, and she must be treated like see fine ladee at all tams. When you get een zee canoe, keep la tete down for the head she make for balance. Both hands on see gunnels also holding zee paddle and then put zee foot 'toe-in'* in zee centair of zee canoe and keep balance and as you go forward slide zee hands along the gunnels. Walk up the center of the canoe 'toe-in' and then get down on zee knees queek and put zee paddle in the watair to hold zee bateau steady while the sternman slides zee end of the canoe off shore and holding his paddle and both hands on zee gunnels steps in as he shoves off 'toe-in' on the centair. He's queek down on zee knees weeth hees paddle in ze watair."

*By turning *toes in*, one obtains a better sense of balance, like a lumberjack riding a log "toes-in" to speed up the reaction to any change in balance.

ENTERING A CANOE

After everyone is off the shore, the guide explains the "law of
the brigade" as handed down by the Hudson Bay Company from
several hundred years past or the "canoe law" dating from time im-
memorial. We gather around his canoe and listen while he instructs. The captain of the canoe is the sternman. He is the boss at
all times except when the craft is in rapids or in cases of emergency when the bowman takes over because, in his front position in
the canoe, he may be able to see danger a split second away. The
sternman tells the bowman which side to paddle, also supervises
loading and unloading, taking off and landing. The pace is set

POSITION WHEN PADDLING

by the bowman, who usually "beats off" about thirty strokes a minute for a four-mile pace in flat or quiet water. The canoe is a safe craft and very seaworthy if used with respect and if the principle of keeping the weight center and low in the canoe is applied at all times. The guide points out that almost everyone some time in his life has turned a canoe over. However, it is considered a disgrace in the bush country. Co-operation of bowmen and sternmen in holding the canoe for each other while getting in and out, plus paddling on the knees and keeping the weight center and ballasted, makes for safe canoeing. Your food, your equipment, and your life, the guide repeats, may depend on how much you respect canoe law, which is based largely upon the law of gravity plus cooperation between the bow paddler forward and the captain in the stern. As a final word, the guide emphasizes that at all times he will show the way and will be in the front canoe while the next most responsible person will bring up the rear. Stragglers often have accidents because their dropping back usually means that their canoe ability or teamwork ability is not as good as the rest. In the interest of safety and morale, keep together and let the guide lead and keep the strays up with the rest. Now let us look at the problem of docking and putting the canoe up for the night.

With a long cry from the guide which is answered by two loons in a little bay away over to the right, the expedition of four canoes and eight paddlers noses out onto a beautiful calm lake that shows just a few breeze ripples here and there. The guide heads for a lovely little rocky island about two miles away where we are to make camp. We planned that the four bowmen would make camp that night while the sternmen cooked. Thus our corporative organization was set up, as is usual on most trips of this size.

Evening is coming on, the sun is setting and the guide's canoe goes straight as an arrow for the island. He keeps looking back, however, checking up on the paddling mistakes of the other canoers, as does the expedition's leader in the rear. It is too late for instructions now, but tomorrow before leaving the island everyone will go through a brief concentrated course in the elements of paddling and handling a canoe; by the end of the next day all will be veterans. Most people have a natural aptitude for paddling a canoe when properly instructed, since actually the principles are simple. When properly directed and practiced, canoeing becomes a habit. This is why it is important to start right so that bad habits in canoeing won't creep in.

By the time we reach the island, the sun has set and we gently nose the canoes onto shore. The sternman holds his paddle in the water while the bowman, keeping his hands on the gunnels, steps out and holds the canoe between his knees; then the sternman unties the rope, removes the tarpaulin and passes the duffle forward to the bowman, who puts it on the ground. Now the sternman comes for-

LAUNCHING

ROLL THE CANOE UP ON YOUR KNEES, BOTTOM TOWARD YOU

RIGHT HAND HOLDS CENTER THWART—LEFT HOLDS GUNWALE

HEAVE WITH RIGHT HAND AND PUSH UP WITH BOTH

TWIST THE BODY FORWARD AND ROLL THE CANOE UP OVER YOUR HEAD

HANDLING Canoes
on land...
NEVER DRAG OR STEP IN A CANOE WHEN IT IS ON SHORE — THIS IS A PRIMARY RULE

YOU'RE OFF! BALANCE UP AND HIT THAT PORTAGE

STEADY THE CANOE WHEN ENTERING AND ALWAYS TOE IN FOR BALANCE·····

ward, hands on the gunnels, head down, "toes-in" walking the cen- ter. After he is on land, the canoe is brought out of the water in the following fashion. The two paddlers face each other on opposite sides of the canoe. Then they reach down, placing the fingers under the inwales of the canoe, and lift up. They walk their hands along towards the stern until the center of the canoe is reached and the craft is balanced up. The canoe is then carried between them up onto shore, turned over bottom-side up with the bottom toward the open lake and the top-side down and toward the shore. This position will prevent a sudden storm from the lake blowing the canoe over and possibly damaging it. Also, it is always turned over to keep the bottom off sharp rocks and stubs. Canoe law warns one never to load or step into a canoe while it is on land—it is one sure way to injure the craft. Remember this well.

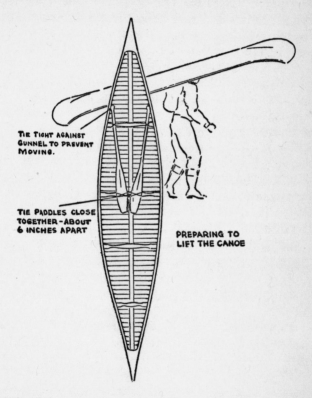

TIE TIGHT AGAINST GUNNEL TO PREVENT MOVING.

TIE PADDLES CLOSE TOGETHER – ABOUT 6 INCHES APART

PREPARING TO LIFT THE CANOE

Now it is deep dusk. The glow of the sunset is low on the northwestern horizon. The beds are made, the equipment is stowed under the canoes and the last dish washed after a good supper. The party gathers around the fire for a little while to talk, smoke and dream of tomorrow. Soon the fire winks low, the party rolls in, but the guide and leader of the trip talk over small problems and come to decisions. Finally, all are asleep, and the little wood spirits who watched us start out scamper through the camp, fanning up the fire and later whispering approval among the needles of the jackpines overhead as their gossip has it that the Wina-Ba-Shoo will welcome these strangers to his realm. Tonight's peace whispers of eventful tomorrows.

FUNDAMENTALS OF PADDLING A CANOE

The first memory of the first morning on the trail is the pungent smell of balsam, and little noises reach your ears—the crackling of wood on the fire and someone busy with the pots and pans. After a good breakfast, blankets are aired and you wait for the dew to dry on the tent so it can be packed. A golden sun rolls up above the horizon, giving promise of a good day to follow. The time has come for your first work in paddling and learning the fundamentals of canoeing.

The party is called together, and the guide and his bow partner launch a canoe while the rest watch. He explains that there are three general classes of paddling strokes—first, the forward or cruising strokes; second, the draw or turning strokes; and third, the less-known jam strokes or stopping strokes. Most important are the first two. The paddle is held at the top by one hand grasping the grip which is shaped to fit the hand. The other hand slides down the shaft of the paddle to the throat just above the blade where it is grasped lightly and loosely so that the paddle can be turned from the top or grip. The lower hand is at the throat of the paddle just above the blade and acts as a fulcrum of the lever. The upper hand on the grip does the driving, with the arm close to the body; and the weight of the shoulder and body is the power behind the drive of the paddle. This technique differs from paddling on a lagoon in a city park, where arm movements mostly do the driving, because in the wilderness one is driving a heavy load and needs efficient driving power with the least expenditure of muscle energy. Thus, the back is held vertical, the lower arm straight at all times, with the shoulder driving the load and giving the peculiar rolling motion and short choppy strokes to wilderness paddling. It really works and is universally used all over the wilderness country as well as in other parts of the world where the canoe is used as serious means of transportation.

With our guide to direct us, we consider first forward paddling or going in a straight line. To go in a straight line while canoeing requires a study and an understanding of paddling—the rest is practice. The bow stroke reaches forward without bending the back, dips the paddle in, then brings it back to the hip—and there the bow stroke stops. Any further motion is wasted energy. This gives a short, choppy bow stroke which is characteristic of wilderness paddling. The stern stroke is different, however, since the bow of the canoe has a tendency to turn away from the side on which the sternman is paddling. After the drive of the stern stroke reaches the hip, the backside of the paddle is dragged backward and outward in a hook or "J" stroke with just enough pressure sideways to bring the front of the canoe back into exact line. The best stern stroke to use, known as the Canadian Stroke, is difficult to explain. As this stroke reaches the hip, it is allowed to pass about a foot, then the paddle is twisted by the top hand until the outside edge is forward and slightly downward under the water. The paddle is brought back under water with an upward pressure on the blade, thus bringing the point of the canoe back in line without any loss of forward motion. This is better, more efficient and more restful. The blade is flipped out of water about halfway back to start a new stroke. The Canadian Stroke is the finest and most efficient of all stern strokes and can be learned easily with a little practice.

After the bow and stern have learned their individual strokes, Paquette tells them to practice together going in a straight line, paddling in unison, keeping the back straight and driving the paddles with their shoulders. Above all, he will insist, do not change sides! Keep on the same side as changing is both unnecessary and risky, and it is a sure mark of a tenderfoot. Later, when we get into fast water, split seconds count, and changing sides might mean disaster.

After practicing straight strokes for a while, we then take up the turning strokes, all of which are variations of the draw stroke. First, the side draw is practiced. The bow paddler reaches out vertically to the side with the blade parallel to the center line of the canoe and pulls sidewise to the canoe. The stern paddler does just the reverse by sticking his blade flat to the side of the canoe and pushes out vertically from the side. The bow draw is an "in draw" or "pull over," and the stern is an "out draw" or "push over." If the bow is paddling on the left and the stern on the right, with the draws described above the canoe would move sideways to the left.

Reverse the strokes, the bow pushing out and stern reaching out and pulling in, and the canoe will move sideways to the right. These are important strokes in guiding a canoe, especially in fast water.

It isn't long, however, before we learn that, rather than drawing the blade into the side of the canoe, we can just rock the paddle in a small quarter circle, pressing down, and a continuous side pulling will result. This is drawing by sculling. For the reverse, a pushing motion can be used by sculling giving the "out draw." Once we have mastered sculling, we are in the advanced stages of learning to paddle. I find that it takes fifteen minutes to half an hour to teach the draw strokes, including sculling. The rest is practice with occasional coaching. It should be said here that the draw stroke can be used at any angle from the center line of the canoe. For a slight turn use a small angle, and so on to a right-angle draw for quick turns, with back of center for backing up the canoe.

Another stroke used, which is really also a draw stroke, is the sweep stroke. For this stroke, the paddle is slipped through the lower hand until it is about halfway up from the throat of the paddle to the grip. Then the blade is extended forward and swept in a wide semicircle outward and back, driving the canoe in a wide circle opposite from the side on which the stroke is made. It is important to note that bow and stern never do forward sweep simultaneously as one would nullify the other. To make a slow turn to the right (bow paddling on left), the bow only uses the sweep stroke while the stern paddles straight ahead. To make a sharper turn, the stern (right) makes a hook or "J" stroke in addition to the sweep at the bow. To learn strokes carefully, study the charts and drawings included in this chapter. You will find that they give most needed strokes and their combinations.

The last group of strokes is that group known as jam strokes, used in stopping or impeding the progress of a canoe. We will mention only one or two of these. If the canoe must stop quickly, the bowman calls "jam" and both blades are simultaneously placed vertically in the water, the blade of each paddle at right angles to the center line of the canoe, with each paddler's thumb locking the blade tight to the gunnel and holding tight to the grip at the top. This is putting on the brakes. I have seen a canoe coming full speed toward shore and when only half the length of the canoe from the dock, the paddlers "jam" and the canoe stops dead still. It is spectacular, but practice it plenty before trying to go at a dock as described above. Other jam strokes are the bow rudder and cross-bow rudder—often called draw strokes—and the keel lock, which is

the same as the jam stroke except that the blade is held parallel to the center line of the canoe and locked with the thumb to the gunwale and the paddle is held vertically. This is done to maintain extra keel in a hard-blowing wind or gale or to steady a canoe at the dock while another man is getting in or out. The keel lock is also used in deep fast water by twisting the grip right or left, causing it to act as a rudder.

The other and less-known stroke is "flamming," so called by the French. It is used in white water when shooting rapids. The paddle is extended out over the bow of the canoe, and the paddler, using a quick back-and-forth motion like sweeping snow with a broom, knocks a hole in the white water ahead wide enough to let the canoe shoot through without shipping "feather water." A difficult operation, the stroke requires expert balance and experience.

This, then, is our practice session after Paquette explains the different strokes: The guide paddles out in a straight line. Then we make wide turns right, then left, by using sweep and "J" strokes, or a quartering draw on the bow and a sweep astern. Then we come back to the snug little harbor of the island, and there he has us practice reverse strokes, paddle backwards, forwards, right and left spins, drawing the canoe vertically right and left, making sharp forward right and left turns. Finally, the party lands properly, each in his turn, each getting advice on his weaknesses and a pat on the back for the things that he did well. When the guide is satisfied we are ready to start.

In the preceding paragraphs are instructions given by the best guides, if they are the right sort. Find out if your guide is willing to teach you before you hire him.

CANOE ON LAKE OR OTHER LARGE OPEN WATER

Since the canvas of each tent is dry by the end of our practice session, each man packs his belongings and his share of the food and extra stuff, and soon we are loaded and on the water. Everyone gathers around the guide's canoe and with a pencil and a compass he orients the map and shows us our position. Then he shows the route, pointing out the main landmarks to watch. He predicts from the high fleecy clouds that had mackerel scales and mares' tails that there will be heavy head winds from the southwest, so that it is necessary to make all the headway we can before the winds begin as we are going in that direction. Without further hesitation, we bid goodbye to our campsite and, with the guide leading, begin to peretrate the unknown.

How grand it is at nine in the morning, paddling along in unison, with the lake and the sky ablaze with calm beauty and the hills lying fold on fold and blending into the green-blue distance! Phil Paquette, our guide, watches the sky anxiously and soon, as he predicted, a steadily increasing breeze is blowing directly into our faces. In an hour it is a steady wind and whitecaps begin to appear. The guide motions us up close, about two canoe lengths apart, and

QUARTERING INTO LARGE WAVES

our party proceeds tandem so that the head canoe breaks the waves. We soon begin to change direction and quarter into the waves, for if you went directly into them the bowman would get a lapful of water about every other wave. In this way, we quarter and begin to work up under the lee of one island after another, using every advantage to break the wind.

BREAKING THE WIND

WIND

On the heavier waves, the guide will give a hard upward pull with the flat of the blade that has a tendency to raise the point of the canoe just as the peak of the wave is reached, thus lessening the pounding; and the canoe will ride into the wave about under the knees of the bow paddler, preventing the point of the canoe from splitting the front of the wave and taking in water. Great care is always taken in waves, either going into the wind or downwind. Danger is also met at the top of the wave, if it is a big one, for the canoe sometimes is out of water at both ends and has a tendency to swing around, heel or weather vane. I have seen canoes heel at the bow and, quicker than you could snap your finger, the occupants were dumped into the lake. When a canoe is hitting the crest of a wave, the stern paddler should keep his paddle in the water to give keel to prevent heeling around. This is one of the advantages of using the Canadian Stroke, because the paddle is in the water about three-fourths of the time.

When the waves reach three feet in height, we work over under the lee of a headland or island and land to wait for a lull in the wind. We lay in for a while, cook lunch, and wait for the wind either to change or let up since directly ahead is open water, about four and a half miles across to the southeast. This would be dangerous for us to cross in such a wind as we would be riding the trough. Soon after lunch there is a noticeable drop in temperature, which later proved that the wind was swinging to the northwest. As we now have to go southeast, this meant that there would be a tail wind. While waiting for the wind to subside, everyone sits around drinking tea, and we slip on our jackets as it is getting cool with the northwest wind blowing. Phil tells us what to do about crossing big lakes. "Nevair venture across a beeg lak if you aren't sure of zee weather. Even eef she is calm, pick your route very careful so that you can make shore in a hurry. Take zee weather, make sure it will be favorable, don't leave anytheeng to chance." His words were wisdom. Later events proved them to be true.

If a canoer does get caught in a blow, he should nose the canoe into the wind, get as low as possible in the canoe, and ride the blow out. He must watch out for heeling or spinning on the crest of big waves, as has been explained before. The best thing to do in case of a storm is to stay close enough to land, and be watchful enough to get to shore. Take the canoe out of the water; turn it bottom-side up, climb underneath and stay dry and safe on land. Few people know the deep caution of woods people against the moods of nature has been built of a healthy respect for nature's power. The traveler knows her terrible power if he is caught in a canoe in open water miles from land. There are just three things to do then—keep low in the canoe, paddle and pray!

Finally, the guide and the leader of the party climb the high rock on the island and study the passage of four and a half miles of open water ahead and the sky for a long time. Every detail of the water, every current streak, every cloud in the sky is carefully studied. It is finally decided to try the passage as the wind seems to be subsiding. All canoes are carefully checked to make sure that the load is secure before we paddle out onto the lake. Careful instructions are given to keep at least four canoe lengths apart, as accidents can happen if a big wave should pick up a canoe and throw it on or against another canoe.

The big thrill is now on! Instead of the grinding work of the head wind experience of the morning, we are soon racing with big rollers out on a wide, wide sea. There is something that gets you out there when the powerful upthrust of a wave pushes you along as though a giant hand were driving you. There is the fight to keep the canoe straight ahead as the roller tries to swing you sideways, and then there is the stalled, helpless feeling as the wave passes on and you slip into the backwash. Then, with a heave the next wave catches you, and so on. Talk about thrills and an increasing respect for nature! You get it out there in the big open water in a hurry! An understanding of the ways of the Almighty begins to filter into one's senses. Apprehensively you begin to watch the sky, and anxiously your eye looks to the point of land toward which you are heading. It will seem very far away. Then there is the odd sensation of heaving to the top of a wave, seeing the canoe which is three or four waves ahead lowering into the trough with only the heads of the paddlers showing over the wave immediately behind them, and of watching them rise up as you slip behind the wave that has just passed under you!

With the guide's words of caution in mind, we do not try to hurry, but just plug along steadily. We are all glad almost an hour later to see the destined point of land get closer and closer. At last, with a sigh of relief, we pull behind the point into a beautiful bay. The sun was setting. We had a more strenuous time than we should have had for a first day, but we were about fourteen miles along our way—not bad for our initial effort.

Lake canoeing requires skill and understanding in handling a canoe in wind, wave and calm. It requires knowledge of weather conditions. Fighting the elements is wrong. The idea is—unless one gets caught unawares—to meet the elements and beat them with skill and cunning, with the least expenditure of energy and at a minimum of risk. The Wina-Ba-Shoo has put us to the test today, and our group wonders what he plans for us as that very night he runs over the miles that will soon be ours, laying plans for his pranks and schemes to test us further. We are veterans now, we have tasted battle, but our respect for the Wina-Ba-Shoo will increase each day as we soon learn that skill and vigilance is the price of safety in a world of sky and water. So ends the initiation of our group's first day in the wilderness country.

DOWN-RIVER CANOEING

Lake canoeing is fun, but it can become monotonous. To have the most satisfactory experience, one should plan a trip for travel on both lakes and rivers. Variation makes a trip more interesting. You can always count on the fact that there will be no monotony in river canoeing in wilderness country. Every bend is a new scene; the closeness of the woods, the birds, wildlife, and many other things add to the fascination of river canoeing. The current in the river, the bars and rapids, and handling the canoe to the best advantage when confronted by these forces, are subjects for life-long study in themselves. Rivers have lured men from the earliest times. They are the highroads of history. They were the hunting-grounds of the aborigines because game could be found in more abundance, and stalked more easily, on and near them than on the lakes. Now let us continue our trip. But first we must study and try to simplify down-river canoeing as much as possible. What are some of its problems?

First of all, skill in handling a canoe is absolutely necessary for the best results. In the river, one uses the strokes used in lake canoeing, plus heavier draw strokes, sweep strokes, crossbow rudder, bow rudder, jam strokes, reverse skulling and all other paddling techniques to get your canoe through. Besides the paddle, one will use the pole and maybe, in the worst instances, a rope to let the canoe down the stream.

Taking each stroke in its turn, let us consider first that we are

swinging down a fair-sized stream in a sandy country where the outward swing of the current undercuts the bank, while the inside
bank is usually a shelving bar. One can save distance, time and
energy on this type of stream by cutting across the corners over the
bars just enough to clear them—and then here is the trick. After
clearing a shelving bar, spin the rear end around about sixty degrees so that the current catches the canoe on the quarter, giving
it a shove forward. Most backwoodsmen use this trick of quartering
on the current at each bend—tacking with the current. It helps tre-
mendously. After working all day, you will find that it will help to
cover more mileage with less effort.

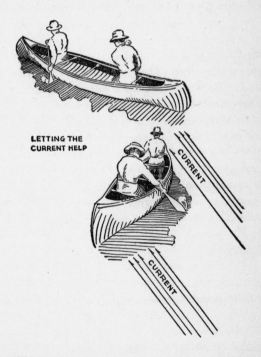

LETTING THE
CURRENT HELP

In a bending or meandering stream, the swift current is on the
outside of the bend, or at the undercut bank, where it is deeper. In
other words, that is where the channel is. The shelving bar lies on
the opposite side where the water is slower and shallower. In sand-
filled streams, the shape and contour of the river bank usually
points to the contour of the bottom of the stream. If there is any

doubt, however, as to snags, logs, or rocks, it is usually best to stay in the deeper water, but towards the middle of the stream since logs and snags usually are found at the edges where logs get stuck. In downstream work, the bowman often takes charge because he can see obstructions before the sternman; however, it is close teamwork. After a few days, when a bowman throws an "out-draw," the sternman automatically throws an "in-draw," pulling the canoe sideways, neither paddler saying a word.

It is a sight to see two veteran woodsmen working down a river, especially those who have worked together for a long time. The most difficult water situations will be worked without a word or change of expression, or without the bowman looking back. It is a beautiful example of teamwork and the newcomer can acquire it, too, with a little practice.

Keeping your sense of direction on a winding stream is also something to be practiced. The direction of the wind doesn't help a great deal—it often meanders up a valley as does the water. Why should it help? Air flows just like water except that we can't see it. Your sense of direction is kept by watching the sun and your shadow; or, if it is cloudy, by observing the movement of the clouds, or, if it is night, the stars. If it is night and cloudy, you shouldn't be on a river unless you are very familiar with it, or unless your being there is an emergency. If it is dark, don't use lights. The rods and cones in the eyes adjust themselves to darkness and in about forty-five minutes you will be able to see quite clearly even in the blackest night. Don't light matches or smoke—this will blur your vision for another forty-five minutes. The Commandos in World War II found this to be true. If you are out at night and think you see some object before you, place your head down low to get a silhouette view, if possible. Enough for night travel, for which the principles are the same on both water and land. Use no lights and you will be able to see.

Knowledge of the speed of the stream is important in calculating distance covered on a map. In a full meandering stream, the ratio of the twisting of a stream is about 2 to 2½ river or paddling miles to every straight map mile. On double meandering streams, the ratio is from 2½ to 3½ river miles to one linear or straight map mile. All streams swing some, even those in rocky beds. By watching your direction constantly or by watching some landmark ahead and by maintaining a steady pace, and if the current is 3 miles per hour and you are paddling 4 miles per hour, and if it is a meandering stream of about a ratio of three to one, you can calculate your straight-line distance. As for example:

Paddling speed,   4 miles per hour
Current,   3 miles per hour
_____

Total river distance,   7 miles ÷ 3 ratio of meandering
                             (Curve of river 3 to 1)

equals 2.33 1/3 miles covered straight-line in one hour.

It takes more than 10½ hours of steady paddling to go 25 miles in a straight line in a meandering stream at the above ratio. If the sections (often called townships) are 6 miles square on the map and the general direction of the river is east and west or north and south, or in other words, going directly across the section, it will take about 2½ hours. If the sections are 10 miles on the side (many parts of Canadian sections are 10 miles square), it will take about 4 hours and 15 minutes.

It is great fun to try one's hand at a little practical navigation, especially on rivers, since the problem is a little more complicated than that of lake navigation. Of course, obstructions that slow you down, tail wind that speeds you up, and other factors to which the good woodsman is always alert, making mental notes, help you to develop a good sense of timing, a good map sense, and a good sense of direction. Vigilance is the price of safety, and it is safety practice to have your actual position approximated on the map at all times.

We are still traveling, but the appearance of occasional rocks and boulders indicates that we are now leaving the sand country. The mountains come in closer on each side, and after a portage or two around a waterfall, the river begins to get swifter and straightens out considerably. However, even in a boulder-filled stream the channel has a tendency to swing back and forth from bank to bank. Always follow the channel or deeper water. Study the stream constantly.

Here are some of the aids in recognizing underwater obstructions. Most obstructions under water leave a telltale mark on the surface of the river. You will do well to study the water stretching out before you for at least a hundred yards in advance, for on the skill with which you and your bowman read the signs ahead will depend how much you will be eating for the next two weeks; an upset or wrecked canoe usually means loss of grub and equipment. An obstruction underneath the water splits the current, making a "V" pointing upstream. Avoid it! A swirl in the center of the "V" often tells how deep it is under the surface. A round stone causes the water to heave upward, and smooth sharp stones split the stream, causing the boiling look in a rapids. Underwater ledges often cause the current to turn sharply right or left. In picking your course, stay to the deeper-looking water, direct your way be-

SPOTTING THE V'S

tween the "V's" pointing upstream. Keep your eye not just immediately ahead, but a hundred yards ahead, mentally calculating and choosing your course far in advance, as suggested above. Use your draw strokes and keep enough headway to give steerage. Do not just drift with the stream as you do not have the control then that you do when you are making some headway. However, don't try to find out how fast you can go; just keep a steady pace.

Now the gradient of the stream steepens, and the jumping of white water ahead tells of rapids. While the bowman holds the canoe steady, the guide stands up and looks a long time at the rapids. Since he is not sure of its passability, the canoes are landed at the head of the rapids and are watched by the bowmen while the sternmen go with the guide to study the "chute," as quick plunging falls or drops are often called. Just ahead, the rapids swing to the right and then to the left as it hits a ledge of rocks. Then it "S"-turns back to the right again, the danger now being a large rock in the middle of the channel after the second bend. It is decided that after we make a right, then a left swing, the channel being split by the rock, we shall find it easier and safer to go to the right of the rock and up close to the wall of the mountain rising overhead. Then it is a straight shoot for another hundred yards with three-foot white water piling up at the bottom where the swift water shot into the slower water. All gather at the canoes, and the course is carefully gone over by the guide, who draws in the sand at our feet the stream and course to be taken and the strokes to be used. All lashings, tying in the duffle, are checked over, and then the guide and his partner climb in and both get down low on their knees.

The exact position for the plunge is attained by the guide using sculling astern or fish tailing, holding the canoe dead still into the current like a hawk hovering. The rest stand on the point of the rock where the whole rapids can be seen. The canoe poises for a moment, then shoots forward and swings into the current. It seems to poise again for a moment, then plunges forward at a surprising rate of speed. Paddling on the left is the bowman, who makes an "in-draw" swinging the canoe, which angles in the current for a brief second; and then with a powerful forward stroke the canoe shoots away from the ledge and across the raging water to the center. As quickly as it can be told here, the river veers to the right away from another rocky ledge. As planned, the bow makes a powerful sweep while the sternman, paddling on the left, makes a powerful push-over or "out-draw," quickly followed by a powerful forward stroke. The canoe now races like mad, the guide "fish-tails" or back sculls, fighting for position. And when it is properly aimed, the canoe shoots to the right wall of the mountain, passing the rock in the middle, then plunges the last hundred yards through the white water. The quarter of a mile took only a little more than a minute to negotiate, but one never knows how long a minute can be until he is fighting for survival in a river gone mad.

Our guide takes a fifty-foot coil of rope and stands at a vantage point while each canoe in turn shoots through. It should always be remembered that in short rapids like this, one takes turns going through so that if one canoe gets caught, a second canoe won't pile up on it. Double underscore the following sentence in your memory. *If there is any doubt whatsoever about a rapids, run no risk. Unload and carry around it.* Smashed canoes are hard to repair, and you can lose your grub very easily. I know, for once I traveled over sixty-five hard portages for ten days with a large party, each day eating one pancake and drinking some tea because two canoes were lost and with them most of the grub. And we almost lost a man. Carry around—don't run risks. It isn't worth it!

Now the stream is full of rocks and boulders, and we plunge along so tortuously that poles are out to let each canoe downstream. These poles are cleaned of all the stubs to make them smooth. Then the sternman stands with his left foot forward "toe-in," braced against the spreader or thwart, and his right foot back "toe-in," bending a little at the knee. The bow paddler, in this instance, continues to paddle on the left side while the sternman uses the pole on the right. The technique would be different if the canoe were going upstream as then both occupants would work on the same side when poling.

To slow the canoe so that it can be shoved right or left between boulders, the pole is dragged, or in other words shoved into the water about forty-five degrees back. With the right arm hooked over the pole and the left shoving upward, the paddler scrapes the pole along the bottom of the stream, putting on the brakes. Every now and then it is brought up, or given a shove right or left which guides the canoe through the rocks. As the bottom gets more gravelly, one starts "snubbing" the canoe to impede its forward surge because of the fast water. To snub a canoe, remove the pole from the drag astern (described above) and shove it into the bottom forward. Be well braced for the entire weight of the canoe will hit the pole with a jolt. Then, by steady pressure, ease the canoe up until the pole is vertical; next, take another snub, and another, thus letting the canoe slowly down the fast water. Steering with a pole is a technique that can be picked up readily. By outward or inward pressure on the pole, and with cooperation from the bow paddler, the sternman can let a canoe down slowly through dangerous water. This method is often necessary in plying through fast water among boulders since it is impossible to portage around in boulder country where the fast water sometimes stretches for miles.

It should be pointed out here that the pole can be replaced for short stretches by back sculling or fish-tailing with the paddle. But these last two methods demand powerful arms, a strong back, and a great deal of skill and experience. I have seen guides come down a rapids and suddenly stand stock still for a few moments by "back sculling," then move to the right or left and sweep past an obstruction to stop again, and again move down through a rapids. This is canoemanship at its best, but only for the strong, experienced and skilled.

SNUBBING

SNUBBING DOWNSTREAM IN SWIFT WATER KNEES BENT AND BRACED AGAINST THWART, FEET TOED IN FOR BALANCE

The gradient of our stream increases, it begins to be combed by sharp ridges of rock. Since the mountain wall is steep, the only thing to do is to let the canoes down by ropes. The canoes are brought to the right bank. One end of a fifty-foot or more line of rope is tied about three feet from the bow on the near side, just forward of the front seat, while the other end is tied about three feet from the stern on the near side, just forward of the stern seat. The bowman walks a little ahead with the pole to shove the canoe off shore while the sternman with the rope looping ashore will guide the canoe around rocks and obstructions by pulling first the bow rope and then the stern rope. By pulling the rope the current is played—by angling against the near side and forcing the canoe out into the stream, or doing the reverse and bringing it back toward shore.

Past these rips, the river, now deep in the hills, slides down
more smoothly, though it is still swift. Our party begins to paddle
again. The sunlight high above, touching the tops of the mountains, shows the golden color of approaching evening. It catches the
trunks of the big white pines away up yonder, giving them a red-
dish tinge; while down here in the deep valley with its high rocky
walls, a purple haze is creeping over distant hills, as in a painting by
Maxfield Parrish, and a cool wet breath of a breeze comes up the
river canyon. In a few minutes we come to our goal for the day—
another large stream converging with our river from the left. This
is a turning point in our trip, for tomorrow we will work up this
latter stream for several days into some fine trout fishing country.
Tomorrow we shall learn the mysteries of up-river canoeing. A
trout splashes in a swirling pool just out from our camp. We un-
limber our fly rods, for we wish to have speckled trout for breakfast.

What scenery and beauty, what a country, and what a paradise
in which to fish! The next section of the chapter is long, so please
excuse me while I go down and catch that fish and several of his
buddies.

UP-RIVER CANOEING

Morning on a river has been the theme of poets for ages. This
morning finds us deep in the folds of granite hills that press in
close. We are camping on a point at the junction of two rivers
that swirl silently together, joining forces to plunge on through the
wilderness. High above on the right the first rays of the morning
sun are caught in the tops of the pines that cling to the rugged granite mountains. Here below, the damp, sweet breath of the valley
brushes the face like the cool hands of a beautiful lady. There is a
tranquil peace that causes one to listen and look, and breathe in
the cool, deep fragrance of morning.

Lakes are beautiful, but there is an intriguing beauty about a
river that holds one to its mysteries. Once one breathes the quiet
air of early beautiful morning on a wild river, he has eaten of the
"lotus," he will return again and again to its lure for the rest of
his days. And when the traveler is too old to answer its call, he
will sit and dream of those past days, and teach his grandchildren,

who are gathered around him, the beauties and adventures that await them on some beautiful unconquered stream in some far country. Surely there must be such over the "Great Divide" in the "Happy Hunting Grounds."

The smell of trout sizzling in bacon grease breaks the spell and soon all is action. After the dew is shaken from the tents, they are rolled loosely, then placed on top of the duffle in the canoes to dry out by lunch time, since it will be hours before the sun penetrates down here into the canyon. Then after a breakfast of stewed apricots, blueberry pancakes, syrup, fried speckled trout and coffee, we gather for a conference before starting. The guide again urges us to respect the power of the river. He points to huge boulders tossed up like pebbles on the point where we are camping. He calls attention to huge scars ten and fifteen feet up on the trunks of the big pines behind your camp where ice had gouged the trees in the madness of a spring thaw a few months before. He throws a stick out on the river and as it floats down, it twists and whirls about, showing the underwater turbulence of the current. Pieces of golden white foam skitter by. All these things are signs of what lies upstream from us. Then our guide tells us that upstream today we shall have to paddle, pole, track with ropes, negotiate through a steep-walled canyon, and carry around a big waterfall. Above the falls will be boulders, swift water, then gravel—another portage up into a country where the river swings quietly between the green walls of a virgin forest, growing in sand and gravel.

He gives us specific instructions regarding the approach to the portage below the falls. Read this carefully! The bottom of a waterfall has an undertow that will suck the unwary paddler beneath the falls to disaster. When the water plunges into the pool below, it does not plunge outward, for there is a back-swirling motion which causes the water immediately in front of the plunging sheet of water to move towards the falls. This is unexpected and a real danger. Keep your distance. Many years ago I once saw an empty canoe drift into Aubrey Falls on the Mississangi before the advent of lumbering in that region. It completely disappeared. Then we saw it rolling over and over behind the falls. Later it shot up out of the water a hundred feet below, where we retrieved it. Miraculously, it had only a broken gunnel and a hole on one end which we repaired, but we couldn't help but think what might have happened if there had been someone in it. *Keep your distance from waterfalls both at the top and bottom!*

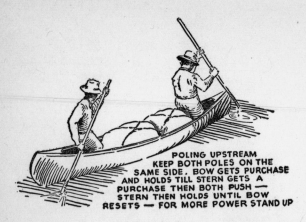

POLING UPSTREAM
KEEP BOTH POLES ON THE
SAME SIDE. BOW GETS PURCHASE
AND HOLDS TILL STERN GETS A
PURCHASE THEN BOTH PUSH —
STERN THEN HOLDS UNTIL BOW
RESETS — FOR MORE POWER STAND UP

Soon we swing out into the current and start upstream. It is a pleasure to watch the lead canoe keep to the edge where the current is less swift, then quarter on the current to come up in back of a huge boulder a hundred feet upstream. Every obstruction in the stream that breaks the current can be used in paddling upstream. As the canoe approaches the boulder, it is carefully nosed out into the current again, and through fast action by the paddler the canoe is "quartered over" under the back eddy of another boulder a little farther upstream. Finally, the water becomes too swift. The sternman picks up his poles and, standing astern, braces his forward leg against the back thwart and the other against the stern seat. They get a good grip on the river bottom with the end of the pole, adjusting it until just exactly right. The bowman works away at his paddle (on the same side), holding the canoe into the current, and the sternman by steady pressure on the pole, moves the canoe upstream. The poler's hand travels up the pole and at the right moment both hands drive down on the pole, and the canoe shoots forward. This forward motion gives the poler time to pull up the pole and take another purchase on the bottom. By extending the arm out and shoving, the poler directs the canoe toward the pole, and by angling it inward, he moves the craft in the opposite direction. In other words, if one is poling on the right and the right arm is extended out from the canoe with the pole angling down under the canoe, when pressure is applied to the pole the canoe will move to the right. If the pressure is down and the pole angling out from the canoe, the canoe will move to the left. This is true of poling done in the bow and in the stern. In poling upstream, one can come up in back of every obstruction, taking advantage of every back swirl. When one of these obstructions is reached, the poler is able to catch his breath, taking a little rest— which the rivermen call a "benny" or a "breather."

Now the current is so swift that both the bowman and the sternman are poling on the same side. They alternate, one holding the canoe with his pole while the other gets new purchases on the bottom. The canoe is moved from one back eddy to another, and in a few instances driven through the rapid water uphill in places impossible to negotiate with a paddle. Poling takes skill and practice, but can be accomplished with a little perseverance. I have won bets in central Kentucky by poling up the sluiceway of a dam that dropped several feet at an angle of 20 degrees. People there did not know that such a thing could be done. However, their cousins to the east in the Kentucky mountains pole swift streams every day and think nothing of it. It takes knowledge, practice and good teamwork between the bow and stern.

The stream has now become too deep for poling, so the canoes are edged to the shore and ropes attached to bow and stern as previously described. This time the bowman pulls and works the rope attached on the near side about three feet from the bow and the same distance from the stern, looping ashore to the one pulling. The sternman with the pole shoves the canoe away from shore, assisting the bowman who works the ropes. The reverse action of downstream tracking is attained by shoving the bow out so that the current quarters on the bow, taking the canoe out into the stream. Then, by the pulling on the bow rope the canoe can be nosed inshore again by quartering the opposite side. In this way it can be guided around obstacles fifteen or twenty feet from shore.

Finally, the perpendicular walls of a canyon loom ahead extending for a hundred yards. We stop because this calls for a conference. We have to talk loud over the noise of a falls booming around the corner, and mist keeps blowing into the canyon. The water is too deep to pole, there is no footing for "tracking up" with a rope, the roaring current is too swift to paddle in, and vertical walls for two or three hundred feet defy any effort to carry canoes around. All ropes of the party are brought together, and it is decided that there is enough in length to reach up to a huge boulder at the other end of the canyon if several of the poles could be tied together with the rope. Three men started on a mountain climbing expedition, and an hour later they appear at the head of the canyon. The ropes are tied end to end, then the ends of the rope are attached, to poles to give more length. These are floated down the roaring stream. After the poles are secured, they are tied to the bow of the first canoe. When all is ready, the line is pulled while the canoe is edged through the canyon by a paddler until he and the craft are secure behind the rock at the canyon's head. The canoe is immediately unloaded and carried up to safety. Each canoe in its turn is tied on to the lines and heaved up in like manner.

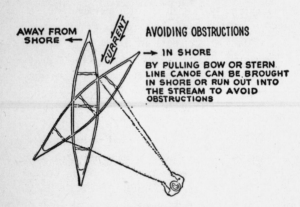

AWAY FROM SHORE ←   CURRENT   AVOIDING OBSTRUCTIONS

→ IN SHORE

BY PULLING BOW OR STERN LINE CANOE CAN BE BROUGHT IN SHORE OR RUN OUT INTO THE STREAM TO AVOID OBSTRUCTIONS

Now we stand and gaze with awe at a huge lunging waterfall—there is nothing more awe-inspiring in nature—some two hundred yards upstream. Rainbows scintillate in the sun, and mist drenches us. From here we reload and carefully edge our canoes up to the portage trail on the right-hand side.

The trail is almost perpendicular for a distance of a quarter of a mile up a gully filled with slippery boulders and ledges, then it swings across a low ridge for another half mile, ending at a beautiful quiet pool far above the upper edge of the falls. All hands soon have everything on the move. The first crew over carries the lunch and makes tea while the rest finish the portage. Canvas is hung up to dry, duffle is checked over, and canoes are turned over and inspected for scratches or cuts. It is remarkable what the canvas-covered Peterboro, Chestnut or Old Town canoes, or the like, can stand. Fortunately, only one small scrape is found, in No. 3 canoe. This is repaired at once with some marine glue and a patch of Egyptian silk (a very fine grade of canvas).

How quiet it is up here where we are eating lunch! One can hardly hear the falls, although they are only a few hundred yards downstream. Here also is a danger, for very often falls cannot be heard from above. I remember one time when we shot the forty-mile rapids on the Mississangi which flows into the north end of Lake Huron. We wanted to make time, so we paddled after dark to reach the portage at the big falls known as "the tunnel." After a couple of hours of paddling, we decided to give it up and rolled up in our sleeping bags along the bank to wait for morning. At dawn we discovered that less than a quarter of a mile away the river ended and plunged into a deep chasm. Even though it had been very still the night before, we had heard no warning sound. Had we gone on, we would have been sucked into the chasm in another minute or two and plunged 117 feet to destruction.

The rest of the afternoon we paddle up the stream, pole through boulders and later through swift streams over gravel beds. After another smaller falls and portage, we enter delightful country where the gravel stream swings between aisles of great pines. Here again we practice paddling across the bars of the sloping bank and quartering into the current, only using reverse motions from the ones practiced going downstream yesterday.

That night camp is made on a beautiful pine-covered point where the trees are not too big to be a danger should a storm come up. A beautiful stream here joins the larger river. We shall camp at this point for a few days to fish, as this is excellent trout country. We also need to loaf a little and repair our equipment.

What a glorious country! Unspoiled savage beauty on every hand. We saw two moose that afternoon, and bear signs were discovered near camp where they had torn open logs in their search for ants. There were beaver cuttings floating down the little stream, and fox, wolf and fisher-cat tracks had been sighted on the sand bar just below. A Canada jay or whisky-jack is making chatter around camp. Black-capped chickadees light on a limb only a few feet

away. Pine siskins flit by like a flock of goldfinches in their un-
dulating flight. Crossbills fly from one balsam tree to another, making their peculiar peeping sound like baby chicks watching for a
chance to get some of the salt which they dearly love. A veery
thrush sings in the deep woods with its unforgettable resonant evening song. A pair of northern ravens flap towards the mountain
wall over to the east, sounding their queer croak. God's wilderness
children eye you with curiosity even as "An-jit-a-mo," the red squirrel, puts on a great show and chatters from the top of a black
spruce across the creek. Evening falls and the fire cheerfully flickers,
making shadows dance. We are happy warriors who have fought the
rivers and have won. Now we sit in this Valhalla of beauty and
peace. Roaring falls and rapids are but a memory now, and the
fire soon winks out in the great blue-black bowl of the wilderness
as weary travelers seek a well-earned rest. In the velvety black,
small sounds of a waking bush country begin as many eyes, large
and small, look at us, the intruders, but pass and let us sleep, for
all know that we are the chosen children of the "Great One."

So closes our brief essay into the ancient science of handling a
canoe.

chapter 4

PACKING AND PORTAGING

Perhaps the subject most talked about by the new traveler in the wilderness is packing and portaging. Outlandish tales grow out of such very ordinary incidents of wilderness life as "tossing up" a sixty- to seventy-five-pound pack on a tump line or head strap, and then holding it snug by throwing up another roll of duffle or two on top. After a man is hardened up a little, he can carry about one hundred twenty-five pounds with not too much effort. However, to hear the story told in the club next winter, with the teller comfortably seated in an overstuffed chair, the load was a barrel of potatoes with a cook stove on top, and on top of that was placed the canoe with one of the more tired members of the party riding sidesaddle on it, and underneath all this was Hercules (the teller), running at full speed for three miles uphill singing "Alouette" every step of the way. "Bilge-wash" is a good name for it!

Another thing that makes you a wee bit weary is to paddle a fellow across a hundred miles or so of bush country, carrying his stuff and the "bateau," and then at the end of the line to hold the canoe up until he can get under it so that you can take a picture of him portaging the canoe to show the boys back home. It makes me plain tired to see a picture of a man or woman with a pack and

duffle piled high on his or her back. I feel like the old friend of
mine, "Swede" Anderson, who found such a picture dated fifteen
years previous. He was heard to comment to himself, "By jimminy,
that bane a long time to hold oop such a load." I'm always re-
minded of the picture of Atlas holding the world on his back and
how sorry I was for him when I was a small boy.

Seriously, packing and portaging is a case of common "horse-
sense." If you are soft and green, admit it and start by carrying
only half the load that you will carry a little later on, and make
two trips. When you are tired, stop and rest. Serious consequences
can result from overstraining—such as hernias, heart strain, pulled
muscles and a general let-down condition, which can spoil the trip.
Let us repeat what we have said before—on your first trip, don't
bite off more than you can chew! Take a trip that is not too hard or
too long if you are a beginner, and don't kill yourself by trying to
carry a load as big as the one that your guide carries. He is sea-
soned and knows the trick of handling weight on the portage trail.
He will think more of you if you have a willing attitude and insist
on resting when tired. Try not to carry too big a load at the start.
He would rather go a little more slowly than to have to carry you
out on his back.

The "bogey" of the toughness of portaging often spoils one of
the finest experiences of a trip, the enjoyment of the beauty of age-
old trails found on the portages throughout the back country. It is
wrong to disregard the extra-time factor of portaging when making
calculations for the amount of time required for a trip. Plan to
allot plenty of time to the "carry overs," as it is during such periods
that personal physical accidents happen and breaking or losing
equipment is apt to occur. Portaging can be fun if you go about it
properly. Let's look into the techniques of portaging and packing.

Finding the portage is one of your first problems. If you are
on a big lake, a map is usually necessary. There is a story, dating
back to the early days of Canada, about a party which spent two
weeks finding the outlet to Lake Temagami (on the Ontario-
Quebec line), now reached by the Ontario & Northland Railway
and the Ferguson auto highway, about sixty-five miles north of the
town of North Bay, Ontario. This party, looking for the Temagami
River outlet, tried several of the great bays or arms before they
found the right one. Lake Temagami has nine or ten arms which

vary from five to twenty miles in length, and it sprawls out like a
giant spider over the land. There are well over a thousand islands
in the lake, and one often does not know whether he is on an island
or on the mainland. Then, too, some large lakes, like Temagami,
there are often lakes inland on the islands. In such an area, you have

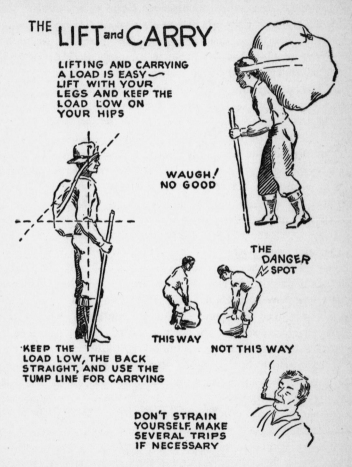

THE **LIFT and CARRY**

LIFTING AND CARRYING
A LOAD IS EASY—
LIFT WITH YOUR
LEGS AND KEEP THE
LOAD LOW ON
YOUR HIPS

WAUGH!
NO GOOD

THE
DANGER
SPOT

·KEEP THE
LOAD LOW, THE BACK
STRAIGHT, AND USE THE
TUMP LINE FOR CARRYING

THIS WAY

NOT THIS WAY

DON'T STRAIN
YOURSELF. MAKE
SEVERAL TRIPS
IF NECESSARY

to guess in the general direction of the drainage, if you have no
map, and to feel your way out by trial and error. There are helps,
however. Often, if in doubt, you can examine the contour of the
horizon, or climb a hill or tall tree and look for the telltale valley
ahead or a notch on the skyline. Often you can spot blazes or mark-

ers or look for the tape grass under the water in the more shallow places as these grasses are very sensitive to current and often point the way downstream. Schools of pinhead minnows often lie in the water heading upstream.

I'm not much for this business of instinct or "sense of direction," but very often your subconscious seems to accumulate many facts of observation that help tell you the way. Many times, however, I have been flat wrong from riding hunches. One summer we were trying to find a narrow passage in a big, high country. We had reached several bays without success. We knew that the big lake was just beyond because the fresh wind in the birches up in the hills denoted open water. By careful cross-checking we finally went down the bay we had tried first and found that an island, standing squarely in front of the passage and blending with the horizon, had camouflaged the passage perfectly. These mistakes are a pinprick to one's ego but they can, if admitted, make for brotherhood among the campers. I know, because when I was stumped for a while and admitted it, I took a considerable amount of kidding from the rest of the party.

Portages on the smaller lakes usually can be found without much trouble, and portages on the rivers are often easier to find since the trails or blazes generally can be seen. A word should also be said about flooded regions. Where spring thaws flood the timber or cause overflow where there is a dam at the end of a lake, the water spreads over the country, creating confusion. Again, try to find the current by signs in the water—such as fish, vegetation, current marks, drifting objects, etc., and try to follow the stream channel through the tops of the trees. These methods often fail, however, and you just have to guess and blunder your way through by dead reckoning and compass.

Portage trails are usually marked by blazes, signs, telltale paint marks left on the rocks by previous canoes. Keep a sharp lookout. Watch your country and map, and you will find your way. If you are lost or the portage is lost for a couple of days, keep trying. It will turn up sooner or later. I will say this of all the thousands of portages I have been over—we found them all; otherwise, I would not be writing this book today.

In very remote country it is often necessary to find and cut your own portage. In the barren lands this is often more difficult, since any former travel is obliterated in a season, and often requires a little exploration. Around waterfalls and bad rapids it is sometimes best to walk out and plan the new trail in advance, then brush it out and blaze it both ways, carefully marking at both ends. If one is in the barren lands, piles of rocks can be used as markers. Brush and clean out well at both ends of the portage trail so a party can land several canoes, stack the duffle ashore, and still have enough room to move around. Cut through fallen logs, clear the trail, then cut logs to throw in the worst marshy or boggy places. This takes a little work but it pays dividends and helps the next party that uses the portage.

If the trail is long and over rocks or is hard to find, as often occurs in big timber, it is best to move over the trail as a group, with one man with a light pack and an extra axe leading and blazing the way. I was concerned about some young men I once took into the bush, and therefore we each carried a whistle. Several times this device saved them from getting lost, and it certainly saved lung power. We happened to have several types of whistles with us, and we found that among timber the high shrill whistle of the pipe variety with a range of tone could be heard much farther than the referee or top-sergeant type of whistle. Bushmen frequently yodel at regular intervals—this carries farther than most sounds. And often Indians use a call, beginning on a low note and ending on a high pitch, which sounds much like the old hog call used in the Ozarks and which carries up to a mile in the open; however, wind and timber or brush will cut down the distance. To avoid anyone's getting lost, stay together; but if one should get off the trail and get lost, he should remember to sit down where he is and stay there, to keep his load with him, to sit and listen and call occasionally. The others will find him. If a person leaves his load and starts looking for the trail, there is a chance that he will never find his load again even after he finds the rest of the party. I have never had this happen, but I have heard of it occurring many times. Take your time, keep together, stay on the trail.

When the portage trail is found and your party is ready to land, there is a definite procedure for disembarking. If the landing space is small, one canoe at a time should land, the bowman, at the water's edge, holding the canoe between his knees while the sternman passes up the duffle. Then the canoe should be taken up out of the trail to be out of the way and the packs placed with it; whereupon the sternman of the first canoe immediately lashes the paddles in for carrying, while the bowman helps the next canoe. To make a paddle yoke for carrying a canoe, one must lash the blades of the paddles about four inches apart on the center thwart while the handles of the paddles are lashed to the forward thwart or seat at the side adjacent to each gunnel. In other words, the blades extend out V-shaped so that when the canoe is thrown up over the carrier's head, the paddles rest on his shoulders. He then balances it up and carries it over the portage. The lashings can be left permanently on the center thwart so that when necessary the paddles can just be slipped in, thus saving time. Once all is ready, the man who is to carry the canoe puts on a pack with tump line across his forehead and rolls up the canoe as previously described. The paddles then rest down on the tump line, taking the weight of the canoe off the shoulders. Then the bowman shoulders his load and walks ahead of the sternman, who is carrying the canoe, to help keep him on the trail if it gets dim. If it is a long portage, stop about every ten minutes to rest. Frequently the canoe can rest in the crotch of a tree, which saves rolling it down and up again. When the party is ready to move on, the carrier can just walk under the canoe and pick it up.

If the canoe is heavy, or if the paddlers are too small to carry a canoe alone, then a double carry can be done, as previously described, by rolling the canoe up on the shoulders of both bowman and sternman with the front and back thwarts resting on their shoulders.

Should the portage be long, requiring several hours, and you cannot make it on one load, then some of your packs, especially foodstuffs, should be cached by suspending them from a limb of a tree by a rope. Throw the rope over a limb, tie on the pack and pull it up, leaving it suspended above reach. Another method is the use of tripod poles which can be cut and lashed, the duffle being pulled up into the crotch formed by the three poles. The best procedure in such a situation is to carry a mile and then return for the rest of the load, shuttling back and forth at each mile-carry until all is moved over. Sometimes bears loiter around old camps and the ends of portage trails and they surely will wreck your packsack if they smell bacon or other food in it, with the result that good equipment may be torn up as well as valuable food lost. If you cannot cache it, leave a man to watch your stuff.

Care of the feet on the trail cannot be overemphasized. Wash your feet regularly. Use good clean socks and good footgear: low-cut leather boots and heavy wool socks, the boots having composition soles to help them adhere to the rocks. Suspenders should be worn so the belt can be loose; pants should be full at the knees and not laced breeches, so that the muscles of the legs can get full play. The boots brace the ankles which will have the extra strain of the load being carried.

When walking, don't step on roots as they are slippery and often cause serious falls. *And don't step* on *anything that you can step* over—such as rocks or logs. Every time you tread on a rock or log, not only do you risk slipping, but also you add to the "foot pounds" of work because you have to lift your own weight plus the weight of the load. It just isn't economy of energy. Choose each stepping place, watch where you are going, keep your balance—a

DON'T STEP *ON* ANYTHING YOU CAN STEP *OVER*

WALKING CAREFULLY

A BROKEN LEG IN THE WILDERNESS CAN MEAN DEATH

slip may mean an injury. You will notice that packers take a short, sure step with just a little spring in the knees and have the characteristic rolling walk of the backwoodsman. Swinging along the trail is a correct description of a "packer's gait." These simple rules of foot care and walking will help your "carry-over" be more fun.

A few words on good human relations in the bush. Don't rush or race through a portage—hurry causes accidents. Help the other fellow. Stay together. Rest your load at regular intervals and take time to have fun, to kid each other, to go over and look at a waterfall that can be heard close by. When returning for another load, take time to enjoy the scenery along the trail and maybe to stop and pick a handful of blueberries. Take a piece of brush and switch the mosquitoes away from your partner as he carries the canoe, or swat a fly on his arm. Give a word of cheer to a fellow traveler coming over the trail with a load. It is the little things that count.

At the end of the portage trail, check carefully to make sure that everything is loaded. The last man over the far end of the trail should make a thorough survey to see that everything is picked up. A sure sign of bad morale in a party is to find stuff left on the portage. When everything is loaded and ready, *all start out together*.

Packing and portaging can be fun if, as previously pointed out, you use a little "horse-sense." This is part of canoe travel and one of the most interesting and satisfying experiences. It helps you test your skill and strength against a rugged wilderness. It will bring you the finest sense of personal accomplishment and deep satisfaction.

chapter 5

THE CAMPSITE

Let us look into the fundamentals of choosing a campsite and the making of a camp. The campsite should be selected with care. First, it should be so placed as to be protected from the prevailing winds, which are usually from the southwest and west or northwest. Therefore, on a lake, use the western shore. However, if mosquitoes are bad, choose an open rocky point where the wind can blow inshore and thus help to keep the pests away. On a river, try to select open places that are as high as possible above the water. If one can't find a good spot, then one must rough it as best he can.

I will never forget the night my wife and I were caught in a deep gorge through which, all that day, we had been letting our canoe down by a rope. We were desperate. It was getting dark, and conditions of the river were getting worse. In a frantic search for a place to cling to for the night, we came on some huge boulders which had fallen from the hills rising steeply above. I climbed up the mountainside and felled several spruce and a big balsam fir, and we built a platform of poles over the rocks and fixed our bed on top. There we slept for the night, with the water running between the rocks under us ten feet below. This was an emergency, and I do not recommend such a site as an ideal place to sleep—

since we would have spilled headfirst among the rocks into the water below if the poles had slipped during the night.

It is good practice to begin to lay plans for the selection of a campsite by the middle of the afternoon. You should arrange to have two or three hours of light, if possible, in which to prepare camp and supper and to get set for the night. In addition, there should be extra time for fishing, recreation and fun after supper while it is still light.

There are several cardinal points to watch for in selecting a campsite. They are as follows:

Dew Level. Dew or mist rises off any body of water at night to a height of several feet. If you want to sleep warm and dry, place your camp ten or fifteen feet above the water level. It is not a good idea either to camp too close to the foot of a waterfall as the mist will travel several hundred feet down river.

Circulation. The spot you pick should be open enough to give a good circulation of air, except in cold weather, when close shelter is sought. Good air circulation is especially necessary in mosquito season.

Enough Space for Tents, Fire, Canoes, etc. You must have enough room to move around. When human beings are cramped too closely, they get into each other's hair. Select a site with plenty of space.

Enough Materials. There should be an adequate supply of firewood, poles for tents and bedding material near the campsite that you select.

Water Supply. This is not a problem in the wilderness country because most water in the wilderness comes right from the lake or river. If there is any question of pollution, boil the water; or use halizone tablets, or iodine in the ratio of ten drops to a gallon of water—each of these methods will purify. Clorox, too, serves the purpose: put about a teaspoon or two in a gallon of water, stir it well, and have it set for about fifteen minutes. Water in muskegs (Sphagnum bogs) is pure and bacteria free. The sailing vessels of early times used to fill their watercasks with peat-bog water as it was found that it would not spoil for many months.

Protection from Weather. Place your camp in such a position as to protect it from wind and storm. Many a camper has placed his tent where he could watch the beautiful sunset in front of him and has had his tent blown into the trees behind him before morning. In the early spring, winter and late fall, when the ground is frozen and there is no insect problem, a camp right down in the thick cedar and spruce is often desirable to protect you from cold wind and driving snow. But watch your fire carefully there, for you might start a forest fire.

Fire Protection. Choose a campsite where there is no risk of forest fire. This is one of the ever-present dangers in the back country, and many a man has returned to his camp to find that a spark has burned up his tent and supplies. Be careful when building a fire over roots, for a rotted root will often burn like a slow fuse for days underground to come to the surface twenty-five or thirty feet from the place where you built your fire and burn the area after you are fifty miles away. Moss and lichens are like tinder —be watchful with them. Don't leave a fire in a muskeg, for the peat moss will burn for a month. If the weather is dry, build a small fire. If it is dry and windy, go right down to the water's edge as far away from the woods as possible, and first build up a shield of rocks or logs. If there is too much risk, don't build a fire at all. Don't go away and leave a fire unguarded in camp, and when you leave, soak the fire with water, then dig it up and soak it some more.

Be Sure Your Fire Is Out!

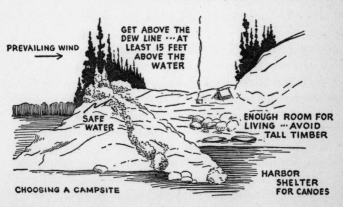

Drainage and Terrain. When choosing a campsite, find one with enough of a slope to insure drainage in case of rain, and be certain also that your camp isn't in a gully or swale. More than one man has awakened to find himself in the midst of a stream or lake because it seemed a nice level spot on which to camp. Keep to higher ground. The terrain is also important; avoid boggy places, and deep black or clay soil. Sand or rock, or the combination of both, is more desirable.

Absence of Hazards.   An old friend of mind, Cal Oswin, once told me that he and one of the Boisneau boys camped at the end of a portage over at Ranger Lake from the Abinadong River. After the tent was up and they were ready to retire, they happened to notice that two big red pines behind the tent had notches cut halfway through them. This caused some worry. Later in the night the wind came up, and they didn't get much sleep listening to the trees creak and groan. A week later they returned. One of the trees lay squarely across the spot where the tent had been pitched and a great stub of a limb had driven into the ground about where Boisneau's stomach would have been. Keep your tent away from big timber. Once on the Missinabi I was camped near a big white pine that was struck by lightning, and the stub landed so close to our tent that the branches were lying against the side of the tent. My partner thought he felt a shock; and I have often thought that we did too, for my gold fillings hurt for a few days, a common experience after an electrical shock.

Place your tent so that it is screened by small trees and is a healthy distance from the large ones. Remember also not to pitch your tent close to cliffs, large fissures in the rocks, waterfalls and other natural hazards, and not across a portage trail or a game trail. Once on the edge of Quebec province near the Abitibbi we put our tent across a portage trail as darkness overtook us. My guide woke me in the night, saying, "Vite, vite, un gran dangere, a beeg moose." I awoke with a start as the guide clutched my arm. In a split second I visualized our predicament. Our tent was pitched across the trail, which we had used as a hip hole. There were six of us sleeping in a row. I could hear the rapid beat of moose hoofs approaching us. As the animal was almost upon us, driving his full fifteen hundred pounds at thirty miles an hour, the guide yelled full blast. The moose swerved, taking all the guy ropes off the left side of our tent, and down it came on top of us. You can imagine the confusion that followed, in the midst of which we could hear the big fellow racing on, his racks rattling the brush. Something had scared the moose a mile back at the other end of the trail, and over it he came like an express train. Game use the portage trails regularly—in fact, they made them originally. Therefore this warning: Don't put your tent on a trail. Something may go through it some dark night.

Protection from Insects. The best protection against insects, if these are prevalent, is to select a site where enough breeze will blow to keep the mosquitoes and flies thinned out. Avoid brushy, grassy and close-timbered places in mosquito season. Select an open place or, if this isn't available, clear one by cutting back all grass and weeds. You'll be a lot happier and sleep better if you do. Keep your food under cover, burn your garbage, and you'll have fewer flies.

On arriving at a selected campsite, the party lands, unloads and brings up the canoes. The guide or leader of the party will say, "This is the kitchen," pointing out an area, "Here's where we eat, and the tent goes up there." Now every party should work out a routine, dividing up into groups that take turns at the chores. One group makes camp, another cooks, another sets up the "table," in this instance the bottom of a canoe "squared up" to make it level (nothing hot must be placed on the canoe bottom). Another group brings in a pile of wood for the night, and a sanitary detail marks out the trail and fixes a latrine and a garbage pit. In larger parties a schedule should be kept so that each will have his turn at all jobs. This is good education and good democracy.

A word must be said about personal belongings. A good method is for each member of the party, after the living and eating areas have been marked out, to select for himself a "claim" or "office," one spot where he keeps all his belongings. This may be a stump, a rock, or the base of a tree. And no one else puts his pack near there. This prevents loss of articles, and the selection of one's office upon arriving at a new campsite becomes a good habit within a short time.

Some people who have camping as a hobby spend a lot of time fixing up the campsite with a host of fancy "do-dads" such as pot hangers, automatic broilers, clotheslines, windbreaks, spring-pole beds and other gadgets. This "fixing" is enjoyable if you are going to stay several days—and a camp grows in conveniences the longer you remain. Such things as a cedar shaving broom, a steam bath, a fish-smoking rack, and many other articles can be fun to make and will challenge your ingenuity in woodcraft. Other activities around the campsite include repairing equipment, doing the washing, figuring accounts, taking pictures and writing in your diary.

One should not slight God's great out-of-doors but rather observe the bird, plant and animal life, and the tracks and trails left by animals in the vicinity. Pick up a moose or caribou or bear track and follow it a mile or two, studying what the animal has been doing. Tracking is excellent training. *But watch that you don't get lost.* Of course, hunting and fishing in season make for a lot of activity in which the campsite itself is an important and focal point. Camp life is the pause on the trail to rest, repair equipment, to eat and to live with yourself and nature. Select it wisely, then make it comfortable and liveable.

One of the finest examples of camping I have seen in many years was displayed by a Royal Mounted Policeman up near the border of eastern Manitoba. He was investigating some moonshining—a federal or Dominion offense—reported in that area. He paddled in at our campsite, slid his canoe carefully up on a smooth shelving rock, and stepped out. As he passed the time of day, he picked out a place not far from ours. Then lifted out his one pack, brought up the canoe to his campsite, and propped it up, and pulled out a small tent fly which, attached to the limbs of a small pine tree, was pulled back over the canoe and the ground side weighted with rocks. He kicked the reindeer moss into a pile the length of his bed under the canoe. With a few strokes of his axe balsam tips were obtained and the bed laid, and with one motion the sleeping bag was rolled out on top. Out of the hood of the sleeping bag he pulled a small mosquito net canopy which he hung. The entire operation took but twelve minutes by the watch. He turned, gathered up an armload of wood, put two rocks together, and with a little birch bark and shavings soon had a hot small fire. He fried bacon, made biscuits, tea and some applesauce (from a pinch of dried apples). Forty-five minutes after he had arrived, he was finished with dinner, his duffle was stowed under the canoe, and he was shining up his equipment as he smoked his trusty briar.

It is characteristic of professional bushmen, prospectors, hunters, and those who live in the bush that they make short work of camp chores, which are only a small, if necessary, part of their activities. Usually efficient, clean, and good campers, these men never waste a motion. The tourist camper, however, is apt to spend more time at his camp building.

In ending this chapter of suggestions on the choice and building of a campsite, I wish to stress the necessity for proper tools. A good three-quarter axe for every other canoe is indispensable, and a hand axe or two will also help. Machetes and big chopping knives such as the woodsman's Pal are coming more into use, and because they are light and easy to carry, they make fine pieces of camping equipment. Of course, a good knife is an essential tool, and other great helps are a roll of small-gauge soft-iron wire and a pair of pliers. Rope, also, and a hank of binder's twine aid in many ways. These are about all the camp-building tools that one needs.

Like the pioneer of old, we depend on our trusty axe and knife, an inventive imagination and our previous experience to give us the skill to take from nature that which will make us comfortable and happy. This simplicity is the refreshing and restful healing balm that puts health and happiness back in persons whose nerves have been jangled by the artificiality and the soft living of our modern civilization. That is why everyone should live close to nature every now and then. They should sit or lie by the fire at night and just watch and listen. It makes us feel small to look up from our little camp bed into the great dome of the sky at the thousands of stars. It makes us feel insignificantly small, and we come to appreciate the infinity of the Almighty. The quiet peace of nature brings us health of body and soul. Let's go into the wilderness, learn to live there, and to come back stronger for having had communion with the Great Spirit.

chapter 6

WILDERNESS COOKING AND FOOD

The remark of John Wabsquaw—"Indian heap big grub, little pack"—emphasizes the importance of well-planned menus and good cooking. It is false to think that camp food is a makeshift and second-rate affair. You need food, good food, lots of it, well prepared and appetizing to sustain you over the strenuous miles. In fact, some of the grandest banquets that I have ever eaten have been of golden brown trout, boiled potatoes, creamed peas, light-brown hot bannock and maple syrup, blueberry pie and a hot cup or two of coffee. Equally delicious is a meal of consommé mongol (made with moose broth), young moose steak (broiled over hardwood coals), mushrooms, baked potatoes, breaded tomatoes, golden tea with a wintergreen berry in it and a slice of lemon added, cake with applesauce or, if the weather is cold enough, snow ice cream. Did you ever have rabbit stew with dumplings or a New England boiled dinner, using Canadian bacon or the lowly but highly-esteemed corned beef and cabbage and boiled potatoes? I love to eat! After a winter in civilization, I show every evidence of it. One can eat royally in the bush country and still carry a minimum of weight of food in his pack.

I remember once when we had some distinguished guests arriving for dinner at a cross trail in the bush. They were from England and we wanted to give them a treat. We planned the following menu, the food to be taken from the woods and our packsack. The table was decorated with flowers and bunchberry and, as we had about twenty-four hours to wait for our guests, we had fun scouring the hills, lakes and streams for certain of the eatables.

Hors d'oeuvres	Tomato juice with smoked fingerling trout Pickled onions
Soup	Partridge purlow with rice
Main Course	Choice of Roast breast of partridge Broiled speckled trout Jumbo frog's legs Fried rabbit
Vegetables	Julienne potatoes Roast root of yellow water lily Greens made from dock, wild lettuce and sorrel (found near an old lumber camp) Toasted Indian cucumber bulbs Breaded tomatoes—juice drained off for above drink
Salad	Cress and wild lettuce with bacon chips and chef's dressing
Beverage	Choice of tea, coffee, hot chocolate
Dessert	Cinnamon bannock and plain bannock with maple syrup Blueberries or red raspberries with cream

After-dinner mints were maple sugar lumps.

Cigars (carefully carried a long way for the occasion).

Our European friends were greatly impressed with what we had brought forth from the woods and a few small packsacks. The occasion was crowned by our friends producing a fine old bottle from Scotland. It was a memorable evening. We were proud of our culinary conquest, and our friends still talk about it, although that was almost twenty-five years ago.

Food is an important detail in the bush country. We still won't go into detail about concentrated, compact, light foods as those are fairly well covered in Chapter 2. Instead we shall outline a few of the simpler trail dishes that are easy to prepare. First of all, before food is prepared, you should give an eye to your camp kitchen. It is assumed that you have adequate tools and utensils, as listed in previous chapters. The next step is the setup of the camp kitchen. Here the primary consideration is the fireplace—above all it should be sheltered from the wind. If necessary, set up a wind-break. If the fire can be built up off the ground a little or placed on a flat-topped rock, it saves the cooks much bending over. The fire itself can be made in many ways, but the fire that I like best is the hunter's fire—by this method, the sides of the fireplace are formed by two green logs about ten to twelve inches in diameter, placed about six or eight inches apart, with the fire in the middle. Start a good big fire, and let the intervening space fill with coals. Maple and birch are best for this, or oak if you can get it, after the fire has been started with pine or other readily inflammable material. The logs should be level and at least four feet long to give plenty of cooking space. Pots and pans can be set along the top of this, or they can be suspended by an overhead pole on prongs or a stick with top end notched and the other end driven into the ground. Use any other gadgets which you desire rigged up to make cooking handy. Keep a pile of extra wood and plenty of water also at hand. And if possible, set up a flat-topped rock or hewn logs as a kitchen table; but if you utilize the canoe as a table, be careful not to place hot pots and dishes on the craft as they will blister its paint or scorch it. Do not begin to cook until all utensils and foodstuffs are located and in place and the fire has burned down to the point where it is suitable for the best results.

Why all of this pre-cooking preparation? The answer is simple. To do a good job you cannot wander around looking for things. A good cook is an artist, especially in the open where more skill is required, and you must concentrate on the job to get the best results. It takes a careful sense of timing to have everything done and ready at the same time so that the entire meal is hot and tasty. It does not require a professional to do the job—almost anyone can become a proficient out-of-doors cook with a little practice. You can learn in your own back yard, in a wood lot near your home or in a park. Try different dishes before you take your canoe trip, always selecting those that can be made from dried, compact foods of as light a weight as possible.

It should also be stated here that your diet can be augmented by a knowledge of woods-lore in respect to edible plants. There will be more about this later under the chapter, "Living off the Land, and Survival." Frogs, fish, turtles, game, edible plants, mushrooms (take care here and know exactly what you are doing), berries, nuts and roots can help considerably. Let us state here, and it will be emphasized later, that no one should violate any game or fish laws unless faced with an emergency or the dire necessity of survival. Obtain a copy of the fish and game laws of the area where you are going to travel, and buy the proper licenses. Even then, use only the amount of fish, game and plants that you need. Leave some for your contemporary campers and for future generations. Let's all help to keep our wilderness areas unspoiled.

Following are some successful trail dishes:

SOUPS AND STEWS   (*can often be used as a main dish*)

Turtle Soup.   Meat of the snapping turtle or of the soft-shell turtle, used with potatoes, onions, and tomatoes if desired. Boil meat until it falls apart. Add diced potatoes and boil until they begin to get soft. Then put in diced fresh or dried onions, tomatoes. Add salt, pepper, a touch of cayenne and a tablespoon of vinegar for each quart of soup, or add sherry wine to taste if available.

Yukon Stew.   Use one can of condensed milk, or dried milk mixed thoroughly, with two parts of water and bring to a boil. Add salt and pepper to taste. This is very easily made and is very sustaining. It was used in the Yukon in '98, and is still used today in some regions.

Partridge Stew.   One partridge—boil until tender. Add potatoes, onions and cooked rice (boiled separately). Season to taste. Note: Wash rice thoroughly and pour off water after boiling once or twice, then steam before adding to rest of the stew.

Squirrel Mongol.   Boil squirrel until a good broth is made. Remove the meat to serve separately, then add pea soup, made from either dried peas or concentrated dry pea soup. Cook until thoroughly done and season to taste. Thicken over a slow fire.

Bean Soup.   Soak the beans several hours and boil with ham, bacon or salt pork, and add onions. Dumplings may be added.

Venison Stew.   Cook diced or chunked venison until it is a good thick broth. Add potatoes, onion, a little celery salt, salt, and pepper. Cook until done over a slow fire that will permit the stew to bubble slowly. This is the king of all stews.

Hunter's Stew.   This is made the same way as venison stew except that any meat will do. Some cooks add tomatoes to hunter's stew. Some omit the celery salt. This is according to the taste of those who will eat it.

Succotash.   Boil together chunk of bacon or ham, dehydrated green beans, and corn that has first been soaked. Cook until done. Can be thinned and served as a stew or thickened and used as a vegetable.

Rabbit Rivel Soup.   Boil rabbit until it falls from the bone. Remove the bones. Make up dough as for noodle dough. Instead of rolling and cutting noodle strips, take a ball of dough and rive or break up into small pellets about the width of the end of your little finger and about an inch long. Cook slowly until they are done, stirring constantly until they sink. Add a little celery salt, if desired, and season to taste. This is a meal in itself.

Bacon Chowder.   Fry bacon chips and brown a few onions with them. Drain off the grease and add to potatoes and onions previously diced and cooked in another pot. Boil a few minutes and serve hot.

Moose, Caribou or Venison Goulash.   Chunk up tenderloin or choice piece of meat of moose, caribou, venison or beef. Cut in one-inch cubes. Boil until almost tender. Drain off broth and brown the meat in a little fat, if possible from the suet of the above. Flour then is browned with the meat. Next put in potatoes and onions previously cooked in another pot, letting the browned flour thicken into a thin gravy consistency. Green mango peppers are added to this if available, and after thickened, add a can of tomatoes with most of the juice drained off. Boil for about twenty minutes more, add cayenne if desired, salt, pepper and a spoonful of mustard. This is good on a cold night. Serve hot.

Chili Con Carne. Boil chili beans until they are anywhere from mealy to soft. Cook in separate pan finely cut beef, moose, venison, caribou, elk, or whatever heavy red meat you may have in the hunting camp. Fry until well done. Add onions and mix with beans, then season with chili powder, pepper, salt. Add a can of tomatoes.

Fish chowder. Boil diced potatoes, either dehydrated or fresh. Add onions when potatoes begin to get soft. Season thoroughly, then drop in chunks of fish and boil vigorously from 3 to 5 minutes.

Creamed Tomato Soup. Bring tomatoes to boil for about 5 minutes. Make up dried milk paste and add water, stirring thoroughly until free of lumps and of an even consistency. Add to tomatoes, season and bring to boil.

SUCCESSFUL TRAIL AND HUNTING-CAMP MAIN DISHES

Italian Spaghetti. Drop spaghetti in boiling salted water and let boil until it can easily be cut with a spoon. Drain off water and place back on fire for a minute to steam. Serve with sauce (carry small can of prepared sauce—not too much weight).

Spanish Rice. Soak and wash rice, boil slowly in double boiler or over a slow fire. When rice is done, steam and mix in sauce of tomatoes, onions, and fried diced meat with either fat from meat or butter added. Season and add a little dried parsley, celery salt, or other seasoning to taste.

Corned Beef and Cabbage. Boil cabbage and potatoes together about 10 minutes before they are done, add can of corned beef. Season and serve. Some like to add a little onion for flavor.

New England Boiled Dinner. Boil piece of ham or bacon until a good soup stock is made. Then add potatoes, onions and carrots. Cook until done. Add seasoning cautiously due to salt in bacon and ham. Serve hot.

Baked Beans. Rinse beans and soak until the skins begin to soften. Put in a ham bone, or bacon, and boil slowly over fire. When beans are mealy (just beginning to soften), add cup of brown sugar or syrup, sliced onion, tomatoes, salt, pepper and strips of bacon on top. Bake very slowly until done. These are a highlight among the fond memories of any trip.

Curries.   There are many ways of making curry. These recipes were brought into the bush by Englishmen with a background of service in India, where curry is a national dish. Wash and boil rice slowly and steam. Add from another pot diced boiled meat and onions. After they are mixed, add curry powder to taste, and season with pepper and salt. Other seasoning that can be added is garlic, parsley, celery salt, or whatever strikes your fancy.

Creamed Chipped Dried Beef.   Potatoes are boiled in salted water and steamed. Add the previously prepared mixture of creamed chipped beef by parboiling chipped beef and thickening with a paste of dry milk, flour and water. Pour over the steamed potatoes.

Emus.   These are made after the fashion of the cooking done in the South Sea Islands of the Pacific. However, it should be said that American Indians have done the same thing for centuries. Dig a hole in the ground. Build up a big fire over it and place some round granite or basalt rocks on the fire. When hole is filled with hot coals and hot rocks, dig out coals, line the hole with hot rocks, put in emu, cover with leaves (avoid aspen or other bitter and bad smelling leaves), then coals, and pack sod and dirt over top. Leave for 2 hours or more. Remove carefully and open the emu. You will have a delicious dinner.

The emu itself is made by placing meat and vegetables in a wrapping of wet newspaper, canvas, a green hide or leaves. Wrap (with wire), soak in water, and place in the hole. I once saw an emu prepared for four hundred people.

Corned Beef Hash.   Chip up boiled potatoes, add a few diced onions (fresh). Mix in corned beef. Beat up an egg to hold hash together. Fry as patties in hot butter.

Scalloped Ham and Potatoes.   Dice and boil ham; add sliced potatoes. After ham juice begins to thicken, slice in an onion, thicken with a little milk and flour paste. Bake slowly until a nice crust is formed.

Meat and Fish dishes.   Fresh-game meat dishes can be found in your cook book at home. These recipes are for meats that can be broiled, fried, baked, braised, steamed, boiled, stewed, barbecued, or smoked, according to your desire. There is an infinite variety of dishes as well as of sauces and dressings that go with them. A book could be written just on cooking game. For instance, boiled moose, deer, elk, or caribou tongue with kidney pie, mooseburgers, caribouburgers, venisonburgers, etc., are very good. As for preparing fish, this is an art in itself. Planked white fish or roasted walleye stuffed with sage dressing can be the base of a real meal. Broiled speckled trout or boiled bass or lake trout are good. Another dish is lake trout with bacon and seasoning and a slice of onion inside, rolled in wet newspaper and covered with hot coals for an hour. This is delectable beyond description. Frog's legs sautéed are delicious. I have found frogs almost up to the barren lands.

These are just a few of many main dishes that figure in your menu.

VEGETABLE SIDE DISHES

I do not need to go into detail here as most vegetable dishes can be found in your own cook book at home. Wild vegetables taken from the woods will be listed in the chapter on survival. Everyone is familiar with, and can learn to make, stewed breaded tomatoes, scalloped corn, spinach, creole green beans, and the many varieties of potato and onion dishes. Look it up in your own cook book when you make out your menus.

TRAIL BREADS, CAKES, PANCAKES

Bannock. Bannock is biscuit dough baked in a frying pan or reflector oven. Sheep herder's bread is the same thing cooked in a "sheep herder's bible" (an iron pot with a tight cover), Dutch-oven style. Pour out in pan enough flour for size of group. (Pint for every four persons.) Add salt, a teaspoon of baking powder per pint, and blend shortening (about a heaping tablespoonful of shortening to a pint of flour) thoroughly with flour mixture. Add cold water slowly. Knead until thoroughly mixed. Roll out in sheets or pat out with hands so that it is not over a quarter of an inch thick. Fix your cooking fire by rolling back the side fire log so the burning side will be under the frying pan which is set down at an angle of 45 degrees. Heap coals in front of frying pan. Place dough of bannocks in greased pan and bake slowly. Reflector oven or hot rocks will do as well.

Trail Bread. (Sour dough can be used at cooler time of year or at a high altitude.) All yeast breads are similar in content, but here is the general idea. Set sponge of yeast cake, flour, sugar and milk mixed together. Put in warm place to rise. When sponge raises (a matter of several hours), add salt and thicken with flour. Knead, put loaves in the pan to rise (keep in a warm place). Bake in frying pan, reflector oven, Dutch oven or hot rocks.

Squaw Bread, Spoon Bread, Hush Puppies, Corn Pone. This corn meal bread is excellent and sustaining food. Although called by many names, it is made with scalded corn meal. Place corn meal in pan, add salt. Then pour over it scalding hot water and mix with spoon until all meal is scalded thoroughly. The character of the meal is now changed to a doughy glutenous mass. Mold into cakes and fry brown in deep fat for spoon bread or hush puppies; bake in a pan for squaw bread, or in a baking pan for corn pone. After scalding, baking powder can be added with sugar and mixed in and baked to give the pone a lighter quality.

Corn Meal Mush. Add corn meal to boiling salted water, boil slowly until thickened. Pour out into a pan to solidify. Then slice and fry in bacon grease. Note: Meat, bacon and ham can be mixed with mush. Some add dried eggs to help in the flavor.

Flapjacks, Pancakes, Corn Cakes, Johnny Cake. All are made of flour or corn meal, baking powder (1 teaspoon per half pint), salt; add dry milk. Some like dried eggs added. Beat into a medium batter. Fry in a greased frying pan or griddle. Serve with syrup and butter. For johnny cake and corn cakes, add 50 per cent corn meal to flour. Fry the corn cakes; bake the johnny cakes.

Tortillas. These are made of a thin batter of corn meal by adding boiling water and salt, beating thoroughly. Drop on smoking hot pan, griddle or hot rock. Bake either to soft rolled tortillas or hard dry tortillas. Serve with hot sauce. Note: This is how pancakes were discovered: In the early days of the Southwest, the frontiersmen tried to use flour instead of corn meal and cold instead of hot water when making tortillas. The result was the pancake that became famous with the '49ers.

Cakes. The simplest on the trail is sponge cake. Separate whites of eggs for cakes are not possible as dried eggs are the whole eggs. This eliminates such cakes as angel food, etc. The equivalent of about 4 eggs, 1 cup of sugar, lemon or other flavoring should be blended together with 1 cup of flour, 1 heaping teaspoon of baking powder, and a big pinch of salt. Mix till batter is thick and creamy. Pour into pan, bake over live hardwood coals in reflector oven or Dutch oven. Icings can be made with cocoa and sugar with a little dried milk added. Jelly covering or fresh berry fillings can be used.

Pie Crusts and Pies. Pie crust is made similar to biscuit dough except two to three times the amount of shortening is used, and not quite so much baking powder. Delicious cobblers and pies can be made from blueberries, red raspberries, dried apples, apricots, peaches, prunes, raisins, etc.

Dumplings. Dumpling dough can be made in the same way as bannock and used as drop dumplings in stews, as crust for pot and meat pies.

Flavored Breads, Cakes. Variety can be added to bread, bannock and pancakes by adding cinnamon, brown sugar, raisins, blueberries, red raspberries, etc. Also nuts can be added.

The above is a brief foray into recipes. One can get many more from the cook book at home. For instance, space does not permit the mention of such things as tarts, gingerbread, cookies, jelly rolls. They can be placed on the menu as their ingredients can easily be carried in a packsack.

DESSERTS

There are many desserts that are readily packed and carried, namely puddings, jellos, rice, raisins, peaches, apricots, applesauce and prunes. Fine desserts can be made from dried milk and eggs, such as custards and bread pudding. Of course, there are the above-mentioned cakes, pies, tarts, gingerbread and others that help the menu. Sauces, syrups, and dressings are found in many cook books: For instance, use lemon sauce, orange sauce or crushed red raspberries with a bread and custard pudding. And so it goes on into infinite variety. Don't forget that rice and raisins served with milk and sugar is an old favorite (this is called "Speckled Pup" in the lumber camps). I read recently about the monotony of diet on the trail. I have never found it so, that is, not if one plans variety in advance, especially in the dessert line.

SALADS AND SALAD DRESSINGS

As long as it remains unspoiled, cabbage should be carried on a trip— if the weather isn't freezing. From this vegetable, a great variety of salads can be made: Cole slaw is one, for example. Some people carry fresh carrots; and a delicious grated carrot and raisin salad, with mayonnaise made from powdered milk, salt, and vinegar, can be prepared. I will not describe salads here, but every menu should carry at least one attractive salad every day. It gives the body nutrients that cannot be obtained from dried food. Many a base stock for salad can be taken from the woods. This will also be discussed in the chapter on survival.

BEVERAGES

We do not need to discuss cocoa, coffee, tea, milk or milk shakes. Tea from wintergreen, willow twigs and other things will be described later. Bouillons and meat drinks can be classed under soups.

EXTRAS

For sheer pleasure, carry a little popcorn. Make a little fudge or taffy once in a while. It adds to the memory of a trip.

It can easily be surmised from the amount of space given to menu presentation that the writer likes to eat. Eating *is* important to the pleasure of a trip. A varied diet can be obtained from the ordinary every-day foodstuffs that one carries in his pack and, if properly planned, most meals do not take too long to cook. Those that do take longer can be done when you are staying over for a day or two. Plan your menu for variety and balance, cook your food tastily and well, and you will have a guaranteed good time on your trip.

The best cooking found in our great hotels and restaurants can be outdone a hundred times next to some quiet lake or majestic river because you have a real appetite, one which gives maximum appreciation, and you have the added satisfaction of creating the meal yourself. The scenery will surpass any made by man, the little waves on the shore or the wind in the pines overhead will furnish the music—and it's all yours out there, to sit and listen to and enjoy. It is surprising to me how many people, no matter what their station or attainments in life, will, upon probing, reveal a deep natural love for the basic things of life, of which eating is a primary one. Let me cite a personal experience of quite a few years past.

I was seated one night to eat a fifteen-dollar-a-plate dinner in one of the great hotels in New York City. The lights glittered, well-trained waiters slid a two-dollar bowl of soup away from us before we had consumed a dollar's worth. Talk began to bubble up as the animal satisfaction of a filling stomach began to relax the guests, both men and ladies, at our table. Small talk began, and I made the mistake of commenting that I could live for a month on the cost of this meal. This caused a slight raising of eyebrows and a rustling among the ten or twelve guests at the table, none of whom I knew personally. I've stalked and hunted enough in my life not to get caught twice at the same game, so I kept a wary eye on this slinker with a towel over his arm. Sure enough, he tried it again, when from the plate before me about seven dollars and fifty cents' worth was gone out of a possible ten-dollar investment. With a firm grip on the plate with one hand, I made ready to spear him with my fork, if need be, with the other. Like an old bear who has watched you all day for a chance to steal your fish or bacon and got caught in the act, he let go of the plate and beat a retreat around to the other side of the table with a very hurt expression. When I asked him what his hurry was, he looked even more surprised and ruffled his feathers and beat a further retreat. More silence at the table, and then the silence broke, and an Englishman across from me said, "Bully good work, old chap. I've always wanted to do that myself." This brought a laugh, the ice was broken, and I found out that most of these folks were real people.

One who had fished in Maine, New Brunswick, and the Gaspé, and outfitted at L. L. Bean in Freeport, Maine, extolled the virtues of the Old Town Canoe. Mention of the Gaspé caused one of the ladies to tell of the baking done there in out-of-door ovens by the French. The Englishman then told of making Kaffir bread in South Africa and also of a delicious cake from the vicinity of the Khyber Pass in northwest India made of rice flour and sugar baked on hot rocks heated by dried camel's dung. And so the conversation became interesting. A lady from Tennessee told how to make "hush puppies" of scalded corn meal and salt, fried in hot fat, and eaten with fried catfish. When the Englishman mentioned bannock, I began to stick up my ears, for that is the universal bread of the North American bush country, except in the far North West Territories and Yukon region where sour dough is used. I discovered that under this polite outer covering there ticked a warm feeling for the simple life, and that most people love the basic things that have made America, Canada, and England great nations. Afterward the austere Englishman and I were to meet again and become good friends. I found that we had traveled in some of the same canoe country.

The waiter slipped carefully back with our coffee and dessert, and I noticed that my parfait did not have a strawberry on top as the others did. This was retribution, but I had fun anyway and so did the rest of the folks at the table. The fisherman, the Englishman, and I excused ourselves, spent a pleasant half hour in the smoking room over some good cigars talking of fishing and canoeing, and had the pleasure of missing the guest speaker's opinions as to what was wrong with the United States and the world. Strange it may be, but I like my own country and have found Canada also to be a mighty fine place in which to live. We three in the smoking room decided what was wrong with the speaker, namely, that he was too well padded, and that he could straighten out his thinking a great deal if he got out into a wide, wide country with no companion but himself and lived with the "great silence" for a while. He should, we maintained, paddle his own canoe, cook his own grub, and have time really to think.

The mention of grub, however, brings me back to the subject of this chapter. In closing, let me emphasize again the importance of a balanced, well-planned menu containing a wide variety of well-cooked, appetizing dishes. Napoleon said, "An army fights on its stomach." In the same way, a bush trip moves on the things that you stow away in the human boiler, things that make the toil of paddling and portaging a pleasure. Good cooking and eating often means a good trip.

chapter 7

FINDING YOUR WAY

There are times in a woodsman's life when he has paddled all day through new country, kept his party happy, fed them, put them to bed, and then sat by the fire half the night poring over a tattered blueprint map, trying to figure out where he is and how to find his way out. The confidence which the bush traveler has in his guide causes the latter to have a deep feeling of responsibility towards his party, especially if he is finding his way through new and wild country. It has always been found best to instruct every member of the party in careful detail about the expected route and the general direction of travel. If it is new country, the woodsman should always frankly tell all the campers that they will have to navigate, calculate, and work out the unknown aspects of the trip together. This is a much better method than to keep them guessing. It adds to the adventure and education of those making the trip, and teaches them a great deal more about finding their way through a new country. New horizons still are a powerful loadstone to attract human imagination.

If you are going on a wilderness trip, you should acquaint yourself with the physiographic essentials (the lay of the land) which are required for your journey and for your protection.

Among these are a knowledge of the geographical position and re-
lated phenomena of the region of your destination; of the use of the
compass; of map reading, especially for measuring distances; and of
finding your way by the use of landmarks, hindsight, and trail signs.

GEOGRAPHICAL POSITION

The basic requirement of wilderness canoe camping is to de-
termine the relative geographical position of the section in which
you will travel and, thus, your own position on the earth's surface.
If your destination is the wilderness region of Canada, for instance,
you must know that this country is located in the north half of the
Northern Hemisphere approximately 45° north to 0° north latitude, and in the Western Hemisphere from approximately 50° longitude west Greenwich to 140° west longitude.

In this particular area of the earth there are also recurring geographical phenomena you can depend on in calculating your position or direction. For example, the earth's rotation is east, and the
sun in the summer months in Canada rises in the northeast and
sets in the northwest. It sets farthest north on the twenty-first day
of June, moving down easterly as the summer advances; in other
words, the farther north one travels in the month of June, the
nearer the sun rises and sets to the north. At approximately the
Arctic Circle the sun does not set at all at this time of year—hence,
the midnight sun. This knowledge, plus a little observation and
practice, will help you to compute your direction from the sun. A
cardinal point to remember is that the sun rises in the east and sets
in the west; that it is directly south at noon when shadows fall
north. If you as a camper are traveling north at night, you will
observe that the farther north you travel, the higher the North (or
Pole) Star rises towards the zenith; the opposite is true if you are
traveling south. Stars are always helpful in pointing your way. Another important thing to know is that the Northern Hemisphere is
in the zone of the westerly winds, which means simply that the majority of the winds blow from a general westerly direction. Thus,
to amplify—when walking or paddling in a region that is new to
you, remember that the direction of your shadow, or the North
Star, or the winds and the cloud movements are all essential in maintaining your sense of direction.

I will never forget the day when a party of us were making a portage around a big rapids on the Mississangi up near Bark Lake. The river took an unexpected twist, and when we counted noses at the end of the trail, two men were missing. This is a serious situation in the wilderness country, so the guide, Cal Oswin, and I instructed the rest of the party to make camp, to keep a large fire going, and at regular intervals to throw green brush on it in order to make as much smoke as possible. Above all, no one was to leave the campsite until we returned. We gave instructions for the signals we wanted used after dark—blowing a whistle at set intervals of five minutes and at the same time striking a dead pine with the blunt end of an axe (the latter is the old Indian signal). Both sounds carry a long way at night, and timing the signals exactly five minutes apart is an important device because it helps those lost to know when to expect them if the sound is faint.

Fortified with some emergency rations, matches, compass, and map and hand axe each, Cal and I returned to the head of the portage trail to look for tracks. We took the time of day—8:55 A.M. At first not successful, we cut into the woods a few yards from the trail, walking about fifty yards apart. Where the trail made an unexpected turn, we found their tracks. The missing campers had gone straight ahead east instead of west as was our general direction. It wasn't long before we got our own bearings. By climbing a hill topped with a great stag pine, which we marked carefully on our map, we surveyed the country ahead. They were headed east into a spruce swamp that swung in a great flat plain clear up to the horizon. They would probably circle to the right or south, and we noted that several miles to the south where rose a large rounded hill several hundred feet high with a shattered north side that could be recognized. With these two landmarks, the time of day, and the observation that the southwest wind drifted the clouds northeast, we had information enough to prevent us from getting lost ourselves. Thus we started to track them—one of us doing the tracking while the other cleared a trail by breaking branches and cutting a blaze with the hand axe where possible.

Our lost companions had well over an hour's start, and it wasn't long before we began to find the first signs of panic—their duffle was strung among the brush. As we went deeper into the spruce swamp, it became dark, shadowy and weird, the branches were festooned with old-man's-beard (lichen), and huge bunches of reindeer moss on the logs and ground gave the appearance of gravestones. We wanted to run. Soon we began also to discover bits of clothing on tree stubs and on places where they had stumbled and fallen. Evidently they were by now thoroughly alarmed. Two, three, four hours passed and we noticed by watching the drifting clouds and the shadows that sure enough, they were beginning to circle.

Cal and I ate a chocolate bar as we hurried to their rescue, for we knew they wouldn't stop in their state of mind. Then five, six, seven hours passed, and we had covered over twenty miles. Still no sight of them. Shadows were lengthening and our alarm began to rise. These boys were college athletes and their endurance was far beyond average. In their first panic, they had forgotten, unfortunately, all the measures we had taught them to take if they got lost, and they proceeded to plunge on and on, obviously becoming more frantic with every minute. Now they began to show evidences of tiring—they didn't crash through the brush, they began to go around obstacles. Once we found where they had stopped. Thus far our prayers were being answered, for they had not become separated from each other. It was for that possibility that two of us had come in search of them.

If you think you have seen gloom, you haven't seen the worst until you are in a great spruce swamp with night approaching— a million acres of swamp, and one place looking just like every other. Deep in its gloomy morass great owls flit, and the draped old man's beard and tombstones of reindeer moss make one think and feel that it is truly the realm of the dead, and the silent flying owl an evil brooding spirit. In such a setting, we hurried on with an ever-growing feeling of apprehension. Here for the first time we began to call, but the heavy curtain of moss and branches mocked us, so we gave it up, saving our breath and increasing our speed.

At 5:30 P.M. we found them sitting on a log in the gathering darkness. One big six-footer weighing two hundred pounds had his head on his knees, and wept great sobs that rent your soul; the other had his arms around the first, trying to comfort him. When they saw us standing there, they showed no sign of joy, only a vacant stare of exhaustion and near insanity from hysteria and fear. Their faces were scratched, their clothes were in tatters and their hands were raw and bleeding. We built a fire right there and got some water from a pool a hundred yards back, carrying it in our hats. After cleaning them up, we drank water, ate the rest of our emergency rations, and made a tomahawk shelter and bed of spruce boughs. We all slept the sleep of exhaustion.

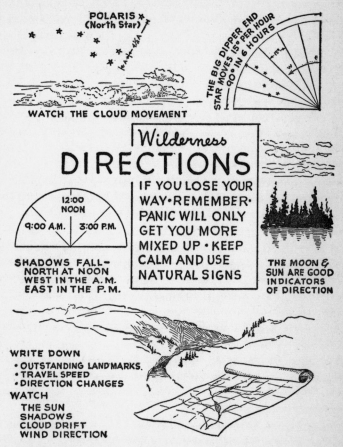

POLARIS (North Star)

THE BIG DIPPER END STAR MOVES 15° PER HOUR 90° IN 6 HOURS

WATCH THE CLOUD MOVEMENT

Wilderness DIRECTIONS

IF YOU LOSE YOUR WAY·REMEMBER· PANIC WILL ONLY GET YOU MORE MIXED UP · KEEP CALM AND USE NATURAL SIGNS

12:00 NOON
9:00 A.M. 3:00 P.M.

SHADOWS FALL— NORTH AT NOON WEST IN THE A.M. EAST IN THE P.M.

THE MOON & SUN ARE GOOD INDICATORS OF DIRECTION

WRITE DOWN
• OUTSTANDING LANDMARKS.
• TRAVEL SPEED
• DIRECTION CHANGES
WATCH
THE SUN
SHADOWS
CLOUD DRIFT
WIND DIRECTION

At two o'clock the next day we arrived back in camp, much to the relief of the rest of the party. We had been gone a little over twenty-nine hours. The fortunate results of our trip out and back had been made possible only by watching the sun and the wind, taking bearings and using our compass; our various observations had helped us to keep our direction, and a knowledge of woodcraft and tracking had done the rest. We passed around the word for everyone to keep up the morale of the two lost men with a lot of singing, fun, and wisecracks. For a long time, however, their eyes reflected their experience.

Recently I read an article in one of the leading men's magazines which stated that it wasn't necessary to take a guide into the wilderness country. If the writer had been with us that day and had seen the look in the eyes of those grown men who were lost, he would realize the folly of such dangerous advice. Many people use the main beaten track and get overconfident, thinking wilderness travel is easy. But back off the beaten trails, when you come face to face with the task of "feeling" your way along, it is an entirely different story. The old adage that "a little knowledge is a dangerous thing" is true. *Always take a guide with you.*

USE OF THE COMPASS

The second major consideration in keeping one's direction is knowledge of the use of the compass. Every person should become familiar with a compass, learn how to sight, read, and record its information. Four main directions are indicated on a compass—the cardinal direction which is north, and south, east, and west. Halfway between each of these points are the northeast, southeast, southwest, and northwest positions. These are enough for the amateur to know. For the north-northeast position, for example, one can look for the point halfway between north and northeast; however, there is a better way to read a compass. Compasses are read clockwise or, in other words, from north to east to south to west. Along the margin of good compasses are marked the degrees—360 degrees in the complete circle. Instead of calling them degrees, the word "azimuth" is used. Therefore, azimuth 90, which means that it is 90 degrees east of north, is the east position on the compass. Azimuth 135 is southeast; azimuth 180 is south; azimuth 181 is one degree west of south, etc. By using the azimuth reading, exact direction can be obtained.

Correction of the compass for magnetic declination is also necessary for accuracy. Before you enter a country or some unfamiliar region, check the magnetic declination for that area. Sometimes it varies from 10 to 20 degrees, and in some spots in Canada almost

30 degrees. Another thing to bear in mind is that it varies year to year. The general zero declination line or, in other words, the imaginary line at which the true north and magnetic north coincide, extends in a north-south direction, bending westward from Indiana through the northern tip of Lake Michigan across Lake Superior and on towards Great Slave Lake in the North West Territories of Canada. Check your declination (magnetic variation from true north) before you start, especially if you are going to do prospecting, timber-cruising, or mapping. If you are using a good map, the declination is usually worked on the map at the compass marker.

MAP READING

The third and next step is reading your map correctly. It should be stated here that most maps of the wilderness country are still very sketchy, even those which are issued by the Government. Mining and geological maps tend to be the most accurate, at least as far as shore lines are concerned. Now, to read a map properly. . . . First, the map must be oriented or placed in a position so that its north, south, east and west directions coincide with the same points on the compass. Then face in the direction you plan to go, paying no attention to the position of the print on the map (the top of a map is always north). Thus, if you were traveling south, the print on an oriented map would be upside down; but this does not matter because you are reading bays, streams, hills, landmarks and not words. Keep your map on a pack in front of you as you paddle, oriented with your compass. Mark on the map any changes necessary: any outstanding landmarks, good campsites, good fishing spots, reefs, rapids and portages. These will help you, as well as others, in the future. Also keep a log or record of the same changes and "finds" each day. Over the years you will accumulate an astonishing amount of information about the country by compiling such a log of your trips.

In map reading, too, there is the problem of distance calculation. Every good map has a scale which shows to what extent the relative size of the map compares with the actual area encompassed. Many maps have section lines, the section being six miles square. This is usually a scale of six miles to one inch. As one goes farther north, the section lines are found to be ten miles square. Scale and section lines aid in your distance calculation. Knowing that your average paddling speed is about four miles an hour on a lake on a quiet day when you use a thirty-five- to forty-two-beat-per-minute paddling stroke, you can, by timing, compute the distance traveled. After several years of practice, this becomes automatic, and a person learns to calculate wind, current, and change of direction until he can estimate time and distance to an amazing degree of accuracy.

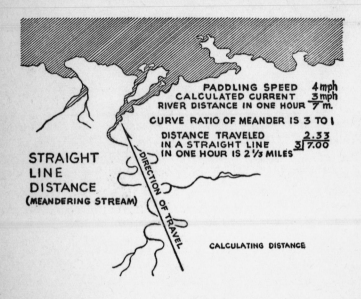

PADDLING SPEED   4 mph
CALCULATED CURRENT   3 mph
RIVER DISTANCE IN ONE HOUR   7 m.

CURVE RATIO OF MEANDER IS 3 TO 1

DISTANCE TRAVELED
IN A STRAIGHT LINE   2.33
IN ONE HOUR IS 2 ⅓ MILES   3⟌7.00

STRAIGHT LINE DISTANCE (MEANDERING STREAM)

DIRECTION OF TRAVEL

CALCULATING DISTANCE

FINDING YOUR WAY

As indicated, the fourth point, finding your way, involves water-distance calculation, timing, and a constant watchful attitude which is alert to such things as direction of the wind, cloud movement, wind drift of your canoe, landmarks, flight of birds, weather, contour of bays, streams joining on your route, beaver dams, campsites, trappers' cabins, blazes, swamps, hills, reefs, points of land, islands, odd-shaped trees, rocks and many other marks along the way. Underwater evidence, as pointed out before, also aid in indicating the direction of currents toward lake outlets, evidences being tape grass, reeds, minnows, sticks, etc. The skyline is also important. Folding hills and valleys denote streams, and the shape of these hills often denotes the direction of the flow of the streams.

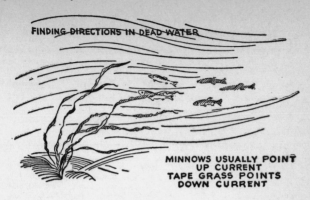

FINDING DIRECTIONS IN DEAD WATER

MINNOWS USUALLY POINT
UP CURRENT
TAPE GRASS POINTS
DOWN CURRENT

Trees, too, help in maintaining a sense of direction, for the tops of trees usually point or lean eastward, being bent by the regular west winds. Other signs to notice are: the tall blue lettuce leaves usually point east and west; the growth of limbs on a tree in the open is usually heaviest on the south side; the pileated woodpecker holes are usually on the east side of a big pine; also, tree shadows fall north at noon, west in the morning and east in the evening, thereby not only giving you the direction, but also

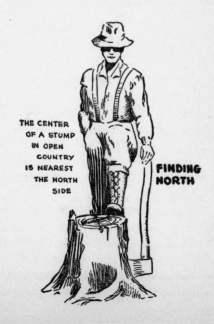

THE CENTER
OF A STUMP
IN OPEN
COUNTRY
IS NEAREST
THE NORTH
SIDE

FINDING
NORTH

telling you the time of day. (If the day is dark, a small stick on your polished thumbnail will cast a faint shadow.)

OBSERVING THE SKYLINE

WATCH FOR THE PASSAGE
FROM BIG LAKES, THE NOTCH
IN THE SKYLINE ··· HOWEVER
THIS IS NOT ALWAYS TRUE

All signs mentioned are automatically recorded by an experienced woodsman, giving him the so-called sense of direction. At night, of course, such stars as the North Star, the Great Bear, and others are of value in timing and orienting. Knowing the trail and country is itself a fine art. Another art, the trick of "hindsighting," is regularly practiced by all out-of-doors men—for by looking back regularly, they learn to know how the trail would look should they have to backtrack, a piece of knowledge they can apply also to **a** return over the same trail on another trip.

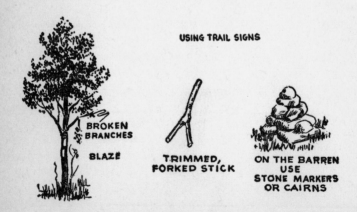

USING TRAIL SIGNS

BROKEN
BRANCHES

BLAZE

TRIMMED,
FORKED STICK

ON THE BARREN
USE
STONE MARKERS
OR CAIRNS

Finding your way is fun and real adventure in wild country. Obtain the best maps you can find, a good compass, and a good guide. Before you go into the bush country, practice—near your home, or while hunting or fishing, or just out walking—watching your shadow, the direction of the wind, and the many other techniques that go into making you alert to time, direction, and distance. It's fun, and later it will help you in a thousand ways.

chapter 8

LIVING OFF THE LAND, AND SURVIVAL

One of the essential things that should be considered by those whose instincts call them to wilderness areas, is to try to foresee and to be prepared for emergencies in event of the loss of food, of accidents, of getting lost or of other unforeseen circumstances. It is an engrossing and deeply interesting subject. The following recorded information and advice is not all the result of my own first-hand "finding out," but is the accumulation of knowledge gleaned from much personal research and the asking of many questions. It is a summary of the talk of hundreds of campfires and hundreds of experiences told by many bushmen. It represents an accumulation of twenty-five years or more of information on survival collected bit by bit from those who follow the dim trails or who cut new ones, for it must be said that every trip and every day teaches new things in the wilderness. The information has been obtained from all kinds of wilderness travelers, native or tourist—Indians, Eskimos, French, Swedes, Finns, English, guides, surgeons, scientists, prospectors, lumbermen, miners, businessmen, bankers, military men, photographers, and naturalists—all have contributed in their time. Each and everyone has something to teach you if you will but listen and learn. Here are the extracts from the contributed knowledge of many.

WILDERNESS EMERGENCIES

What To Do If Lost! First—Be prepared! Carry with you at all times a compass, some paraffined matches, a good knife, and, if on the trail or tracking or hunting, carry some emergency rations and salt. It has been found that a hunk of unsliced dried beef is an excellent thing to carry in your coat. You can chew on it for days and it is very sustaining. Always have a general knowledge of the layout of the country. Carry a map with you, if possible, and always let your buddies know when you leave camp, where you intend to go, and when you expect to return. Always have prearranged signals at your base for use in case you get lost. Such signals can be smoke, gunshots, yodeling, mirror flashing, whistles, beating on a dead pine with an axe or club, or strong flashlight beams directed up into the sky. These all help bring the lost ones back to camp. If you are tracking or spreading out over a country looking for a lost person, remember that most people when lost have a tendency to circle to the right or clockwise. If your companions are out on the water on a big lake and darkness comes, build signal fires, hang out a lantern, or use a flashlight at regular intervals.

If you find yourself confused and lost, stop immediately, sit down on a log, smoke, chew a twig—just calm down for a while before trying to find your way out. Then think. If you have a map and a compass, study them carefully. If you can backtrack, do so carefully, leaving a blazed trail of broken twigs or blazes with your knife or axe as you go. If that fails, then get to the nearest high spot and call, build a smoke signal, fire two shots in succession. You can beat a hollow or a dry dead tree, but you must get on a high spot above the timber so the sound will carry. *Above all, if you have companions, they will come looking for you. Don't wander, stay where you are. Keep calm, call, signal, watch and listen. Getting lost is a number-one danger in any wilderness country.* Every guide should instruct every member of his party in what to do if lost. It is well for parties to stay together, check up regularly, and be careful to stay on the trail. The guide should teach all to watch the sun, the wind direction (usually from the west), and outstanding landmarks, and to practice hindsighting, blazing and twig snapping to help backtrack. The regular use of compass and maps is a must. Know trends of main streams, mountain ranges, valleys, general slope of the land, unusual features and many other things which will prevent you from getting lost.

Another thing to remember is that when a person has been lost, he usually suffers from mental shock. Cheer him up, sing, tell jokes, make light of his recent predicament, give him a good strong stimulant and fill him with a good meal. It will help him to forget and to restore his equilibrium.

Forest Fire Prevention. Perhaps the next real danger to everyone in the bush country is fire. First, take care in building fires at all times. In dry weather, build fires in the open, away from moss, dry grass, branches. Use wood that doesn't spark too much. Keep your fires small, especially in the daytime, and when you leave, soak the fire with water, dig it up and soak it again. *Always be sure that your fire is out!* In case you locate a forest fire, report it if at all possible. If it is a large one, take immediate note of the direction of the wind, get your party off the trail and out onto the biggest body of water that you can find. If the smoke gets too dense, put your face down near the water as there is always a layer of air about six inches above the surface. A wet handkerchief over the nose and mouth helps breathing.

If a fire has started and is beyond control, take a quick survey of the situation and, like an army general in a battle, deploy your forces strategically. If a west wind is blowing, the fire then will fan out eastward. Say that you know that a mile to the east a stream flows north and south, or there is located a road, bay, or an open stretch of ground. At all speed get to the barrier that the fire will have to jump, and along the west side of the barrier start back fires that will burn slower upwind but far enough to have a wide belt already burned to meet the oncoming fire and to neutralize it. This method often saves millions of dollars in timber, and in animal, bird and other life, as well as the beauty that would otherwise be destroyed. Nothing is more ugly and uninviting than burned-over country. Let's keep the forests green.

Fire is perhaps the greatest enemy in the bush as it destroys all before it. With the advent of forestry patrol planes, portable water pumps, and better communications, such as the walkie-talkie and other radio equipment, it has now become much easier to fight fires. Still, millions of acres are burned each year. The best way to fight fires, of course, is to prevent them before they begin by being extremely careful with matches and when smoking, especially cigarettes. I repeat—be sure that your campfire is out and soaked with water, dug up and soaked again before you leave it. Digging is necessary since dry roots will burn underground like a fuse for many hours and the flame will come out to start a fire long after you have gone.

In Case You Lose Your Food. In 1926, at a time when we were far back in the bush, a freight canoe with our grub dumped at the bottom of a chute-rapids and we lost most of the food. The canoe was smashed. It happened that a canoeist who had been used to the Charles River in Boston, against orders shot the rapids and almost lost his life. He also caused us ten days of excruciating hunger and hardship. We came out over sixty-five rugged portages on the equivalent of one pancake a day, tea and occasionally roots and fish that we could pick up. There were eighteen of us and, finally, when they became so weak that they could go no farther, Oscar Boyer and I walked thirty miles to John Macke's outpost lumber camp and packed back a load of prunes, salt pork and flour. We fed them for three days before they were able to go on the trail again. It was an unforgettable experience, and since then I have instinctively collected lore on survival food. At the end of this chapter there is a chart describing wild foods to be obtained in the bush country.

The Indian is a master at living off the land and for that reason he is also a fine conservationist. Almost anything that walks, grows, crawls, swims or flies can be eaten. Of course, some are not as palatable as others, but when you're starving you are not very choosy. Here is an outline of wild foods and how to get them.

Meat Don't depend solely on hunting to supply your meat on any trip. If you are in dire straits, you can snare grouse, shoot squirrels, catch frogs, fish, dig fresh-water clams, pick fresh-water snails, snare rabbits or get a moose with an axe while he is swimming. You can catch mice or birds in several ways—by snare, deadfall or trap—or catch ducks with bait on a fishhook and line anchored to a stake in shallow water. Even the skunk is good to eat. In the North, there are two easily caught sources of meat, if they can be found. First, spruce grouse and second, porcupine.

The spruce grouse or fool hen (so called because it will allow a person to come up close to it) can be snared with a shoelace looped at the end of a long pole. Cut the pole, tie the shoelace on the other end, and make a sliding loop. Wet the lace so that it will be stiff enough to stand out. After locating a bird perched within reach, move up slowly, gently drop the loop over the bird's head, and give a jerk. Supper is served!

The porcupine can easily be overtaken or cut down out of a tree and clubbed to death. Pick him up under the chin and be careful of his quills. Then run a pole down his mouth and hold him over the flames of the fire until all quills are burned off. After skinning you will have some fine pork-like meat that is very sustaining. Grease can be rendered for shortening and lamp oil.

In emergencies wild duck can be caught by small hooks covered with bait and attached to a line staked to the bottom of a shallow place where they feed. Rabbits can be snared or brought down by deadfalls or by setting snares on their runways near spruce and cedar swamps. Bird's eggs are good, as are turtles, snakes, salamanders, frogs, fish, clams and snails. I have eaten all of them.

Vegetables The wilderness country is full of edible plants. The root of the yellow water lily, the root of the cattail. The

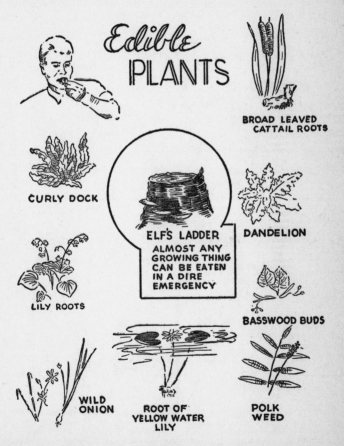

Edible PLANTS

BROAD LEAVED CATTAIL ROOTS

CURLY DOCK

ELF'S LADDER
ALMOST ANY GROWING THING CAN BE EATEN IN A DIRE EMERGENCY

DANDELION

LILY ROOTS

BASSWOOD BUDS

WILD ONION

ROOT OF YELLOW WATER LILY

POLK WEED

root shoots of the great green bullrush are delicious stewed, baked or fried. The buds of the basswood are a substitute for green beans. Wild lettuce, dock, lamb's quarter make grand greens as well as salads. Even the root of the wild turnip and skunk cabbage can be used if boiled and drained several times. There are few, if any, poisonous roots in Canada. However, some can act as a strong purge or physic, such as the May apple root, or as a binder-upper as the Calmus root. Even lichens, young fern fronds, liverworts, and a wide variety of fungi or mushrooms can be eaten. Select mushrooms that grow on dead wood, and you'll be safe from the poisonous ones. When cooking wild herbs or bulbs, it is best to pour off the first water and then cook and season well. This improves the taste.

MOONSEED

DEATH CUP
MUSHROOM

POISON
HEMLOCK

WHITE HELLEBORE

WATER HEMLOCK

AVOID THESE

PLANTS

Cereals Cereals are less common, but there are a number of good substitutes. Wild rice in season is, of course, excellent. The roots of cattails, water lilies, etc., can be boiled, dried and pounded into a type of crude flour. The seeds of the dock family, tick trefoils can be ground into a poor-grade pastry flour. Hazelnuts can be beaten into an oily flour and the tips of the buds of the basswood can be dried and ground up into a glutenous mass substituting for flour. Even lichens give a gluten that can be used.

Wild CEREAL

ROOTS AND UNDERWATER PULPY STEMS OF WATER LILY

BOILED ACORNS

BASSWOOD BUDS DRIED AND POUNDED

IT TAKES TIME TO COLLECT, DRY AND GRIND THE CEREALS BUT THE BODY REQUIRES A CERTAIN AMOUNT OF STARCH

WILD RICE

TICK TREFOIL

HAZEL NUTS

Fruits Of course, the wilderness country, especially in the North, in season abounds in many varieties of fruits—such as wild red raspberries, blueberries, strawberries (in some parts), and many others. These can be dried individually and preserved or crushed, or spread out in sheets and dried, so that they can be carried with you. Indians have known and done this for countless centuries.

Wild Fruits

WILD PLUMS AND APPLES PRESERVED IN WILD HONEY WAS A FAVORITE FOOD OF THE AMERICAN INDIAN

WILD PLUM

PAWPAW AUTUMN THESE ARE BEST WHEN FROSTBITTEN

WHITE MULBERRY

LAY FRUIT ON A FLAT ROCK WITH GOOD SUN AND VENTILATION

BLACK CHERRY JULY TO SEPT. RAW OR COOKED

BLACKBERRIES AND RASBBERRIES ARE VERY GOOD EATEN RAW

SERVICE BERRY JUNE OR JULY EAT RAW OR COOKED

WILD STRAWBERRY JUNE AND JULY EAT RAW OR COOKED

WILD GRAPE

Beverages A substitute for lemonade can be made from sumac berries (avoid poison sumac that grows in peat bogs). Sassafras can be used where found. Spice bush makes good tea, also spearmint, peppermint, and wintergreen; and in some more civilized areas, chicory roots can be dug, dried and roasted for coffee. Wild-lettuce roots and dandelion roots dried and roasted make a good coffee drink. Wild cereals can be scorched and made into a coffee drink also. Tender new twigs of basswood or spruce tips can be used for tea. Wild fruits, such as blueberries and red raspberries can be crushed and mixed with some sugar and water to make an excellent drink. So can cranberry juice and many others. Basswood flowers make a wonderfully delicious tea in season.

Sugar This can be obtained from maple and beechnut trees in early spring. Bee trees often can be found and are a source of sugar and, of course, many of the sweeter fruits are full of sugar.

Spices and Flavors Wild leek or onion is a good substitute for onions. Sweet anise root gives a delicate flavor; sarsaparilla, peppermint and spearmint, sweet fern, spice bush and many others make good flavorings as well as teas. Cresses, lamb's quarter, and other tender shoots can be used as seasoning in salads, meats, and gravies. If there is a lack of salt in meats, char or burn them a little. It seems to help the taste, and you don't miss the salt.

Chewing Materials Which Allay Hunger The twigs of the basswood and elm, the tips of spruce, sweet birch and balsam make good chewing material, especially in winter when food is scarce. The twigs and the inner bark of the sweet birch are good. Slippery elm is good where found and the inner bark can be chewed, lessening the pangs of hunger. The inner bark of the jackpine is quite good to chew, especially in the spring. Clover when found, plantain leaves, sorrel, lamb's quarter, and even grass is quite sustaining. The fiddle head of bracken or brake fern in the spring are quite nourishing. Spruce gum can be chewed, but too much will upset the stomach. Inner bark of maple can be chewed. Sarsaparilla roots can be chewed—they are quite a common flora and contain medicinal qualities.

A final word on wild foods. It is a great truth that loss of food is very dangerous in the wilderness, and if you have to live off the land, don't plan to hurry. Travel slowly and forage en route. Stop in the middle of the afternoon at a spot that looks like a good hunting ground for food of all kinds. Don't do anything unnecessary. Conserve your energy, which means calories, and calories mean food. Above all, remember that as starvation drives into your system you have a tendency to be depressed, pessimistic, irritable and panicky. Force yourself to be optimistic, whistle, and bolster the morale of the men where it seems most needed. Be sure above all to have each man carry his share of the load and work according to his strength. Don't let the braver kill themselves with work and kindness towards the less worthy. When you are on survival rations, it is share and share alike, in both food and work. This is not philanthropy but a "just must" for the good of all if you are to get through alive.

Something should be said about the wisdom of taking enough food plus a little extra for emergencies or unexpected guests. It is romantic to hear or read about hardship, but it takes the fun out of a trip. Plan carefully. Tie your grub into the canoe, plenty of it. Then you need only draw from nature's storehouse as an extra and an interesting bonus. Have full knowledge of what to do in case of an emergency but, personally, I hope you will never have occasion to use it.

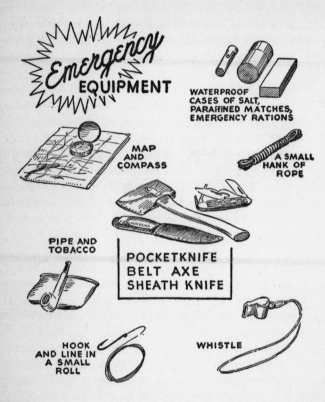

Now let us give our attention to survival and emergency equipment. It may save your life some day. One develops a good, healthy respect and admiration for his primitive ancestors when he, through necessity, has to create his own equipment and clothes in order to sustain his life. It is not any easy task, but think of the advantage that we have over early man—in such inventions as the bow and arrow for instance—who with bare hands and a club had to build his world. Hands and club meant his survival. For your survival, such equipment as axes, bows, arrows, spears, traps fishhooks and lines, shelters, packs, ropes, boats, rafts, canoes, paddles, clothes, beds and cooking utensils can all be created in an emergency.

EMERGENCY CLOTHES

Coats, Shirts, Pants: These can be made from blankets, canvas, sacking, buckskin, caribou or moose skin, bear, rabbit, fox, and other hides. Buckskin, of course, is the classic material to use if deer are available. Caribou skin is better than deer in some ways, but it is heavier. Moose—and bearskins are usually too heavy for clothing, but can be used for boots and moccasins. (Save the sinews of the carcass for sewing.) To tan hides, save the brains and tallow for rubbing and softening the hide. Roll skin in wood ashes with the fur inside. Soak for a week, scrape off the hair, and tan with a rubbing pole and applications of brains and tallow. The most simple blanket coat is made by folding a blanket crosswise, and cutting a head hole in the middle by means of a slit. Put this on over the head and hold in place with a belt around the middle. There are dozens of simple ways to make coats and breeches, and with a little imagination one can create emergency pants, coats and shirts.

Socks. Socks can be made of blankets, cased rabbitskins and skins of other small animals. Loon and duck skins with down left on and turned inside make some of the warmest socks in the world. Pieces of blankets can be easily wrapped on the foot after the fashion of the triangular foot bandage so familiar to those who know first-aid, or a sack-like arrangement can be made and the foot inserted, or the pieces can be sewed up like moccasins if thread is available. Socks for cold weather can be made by case-skinning rabbits and sliding the foot into the hide (fur side in and belly up) with your toes toward the head, and slitting the belly to let the ankle in. The hide is then pulled up around the back of the heel. Temporary moccasins can be made this way also. It is good to remember that Indians, Eskimos and even European peasants use grass and straw in the bottom of their shoes for warmth as it is excellent insulation against the cold.

Shoes, Boots and Moccasins. Footgear can become a number-one problem, especially in rough country. Moccasins of buckskin can be made. Heavy canvas helps protect the feet, and in winter even burlap sacks may be used. The well-known Cree boots are fashioned by case skinning (pulled over) off the hind legs of a moose over the bend in the leg; the skin is then turned so that the fur is inside, and the small end is sewed shut and the foot is placed in the large end, with the heel fitting into the elbow bend in the moose leg. Tough and good are the Cree boots. Sandals can be provided for temporary use from thick birchbark. Wooden clogs can be used. It is always wise to carry an awl and a leather sewing kit with you in case you need to repair or make shoes; however, awls can be created from fish bones, deer-leg bones, nails, etc.

Hats and Parkas. Parkas can be made from blankets, furs, sacking or canvas. And hats can be produced from hides, birchbark, canvas, grass, reeds, vines, and many other materials.

Emergency
CLOTHES

A COOLIE HAT CAN EASILY BE MADE FROM BIRCHBARK

12"SLIT

CUT A 12" SLIT IN A BLANKET, USE IT LIKE A PONCHO

LOON SKINS MAKE GOOD SOCKS WITH THE DOWN SIDE, WARM SIDE INSIDE

CASED SKINNED RABBITS MAKE ...

MITTENS OR SOCKS

BOOTS CAN BE MADE FROM THE CASE SKINNED HIND LEGS OF A MOOSE

Gloves and Mittens. Gloves and mittens are easily fashioned from canvas, burlap, buckskin, rabbitskins, loon skins, owl skins, duck skins, or gull skin. Be sure that they are long enough to cover far up the wrists to protect you from the cold.

As a final word about emergency clothes—if it is cold, make them to fit loosely so that you will be warmer. Take time to make them strong and hole-proof and they will preserve you when you need them the most and prevent serious frostbite in cold weather.

EMERGENCY SHELTERS

Lean-tos, birchbark wigwams (Wig-wom means "bark tent" in Ojibwa) or a tree shelter made by felling a large fir and trimming out the under branches produce satisfactory shelter. Overhanging rocks can be made into shelters. An excellent shelter can be made against the roots of an uprooted tree, for the dirt on the roots can be the back of a fireplace with poles and thatching overhead. Actually there are hundreds of ways to create good shelters, such as from sod blocks and, of course, snow in winter. Another good way is to dig into a sand bank when the frozen ground or roots overhead hold the ceiling. Even rocks can be built up and chinked with moss. It is best to use the material which you find at hand. Shelters can be built, however, in even the most barren places.

EMERGENCY MEASURES TO KEEP FROM FREEZING

In any emergency involving cold weather, in an oncoming blizzard, or if lost when the temperature is freezing and you have only a minimum of equipment with you, you must consider these four cardinal points: insulation and clothing; protection from wind; food; fire.

Insulation and Clothing. This is the primary necessity. Stuff paper, moss, balsam, grass or other insulation material in your shirts, pants, socks, and shoes. Insulation is the keynote. Even rabbitskins and bird skins can be used, although usually in a temporary emergency these are not available. An interesting fact to note here is that good insulation must "breathe" in order to give the best results and get rid of body moisture. Rubberized tight coverings are good only temporarily to break the wind.

Protection from Wind. Protection especially from wind, is next in importance. If you are on open tundra, dig down into the snow, build a windbreak of rocks, frozen moss or snow blocks. If you are in the bush in winter, protect yourself in spruce swamps or deep valleys or behind a hill or in a gully. Build a small, efficient shelter and take time to do a good job. You won't regret it.

Emergency **SHELTER**

SNOW BLOCK HOUSE

UPTURNED CANOE WITH REFLECTOR

LOP TREE WITH BOUGH BED AND REFLECTOR

SOD HOUSE — IT IS A WELL INSULATED SHELTER SUITABLE FOR ALL WEATHER

GRASS OR REED THATCH

BOULDER SHELTER WITH MOSS CHINKING

USE A BLANKET INDIAN STYLE SIT ON ONE POINT-STUFF SHIRT BACK OF BLANKET WITH GRASS, LEAVES OR BALSAM – PULL OTHER POINT OVER HEAD AND ARMS WITH BACK TO WIND.- MAKE A SMALL FIRE IF AT ALL POSSIBLE

HEAT THE GROUND   BRUSH AWAY THE ASHES   SLEEP ON HEATED GROUND

Food. Food is fuel inside you. Get food into you and forage if you have none. Almost all plant life you see and anything whose tracks you can see can be eaten. Keep your internal calories up.

Fire. Always carry a good supply of paraffined matches. If these are not available, a little piece of quartz, the back of your penknife and the shredded bark of a cedar or your handkerchief—and you build a fire by flint and steel. If the sun is shining, unscrew the lens from your binoculars and start a fire by focusing on dry punk wood, a shredded cotton handkerchief or cedar bark. If you have a gun, remove the bullet and stuff with a soft rag. Then shoot into a barrier. The powder will ignite the wicking, and you have a beginning for your fire. Should you have a cigarette lighter, even though the fluid may be missing the wick can be carefully pulled out, preserving the char, and a spark created. Of course, the bow drill may be used as a last resort to obtain fire. Your shoelace can be used on the bow to turn the spindle; cedar bark would serve for tinder; and the board and spindle can be made of basswood, aspen or other soft, resin-free and nonacid wood. Any Boy Scout handbook can show you how to build a bow-drill fire set.

EMERGENCY BEDS

The requirements of good emergency bedding are 1) windbreak or shelter; 2) good insulation over and under; 3) a good reflecting fire. Once Oscar Boyer and I slept for weeks with no other blankets than a burned slicker and a burned half pup tent. We just up-edged the canoe in front of a reflector fire and built a balsam bed, then spread the pup tent and slicker, heaped more balsam on top, and burrowed in each night. Lichens and moss can also be used as well as grass, reeds or any such material. Be sure to use plenty of whatever emergency materials you have at hand. If you have one blanket and it is very cold, insulate your back, sit on a log on a corner of the blanket diagonally, build a small fire between your legs. Drop your head down on your knees and make a little hole in the top of the blanket for the smoke to escape. You can sleep warm in the coldest of weather in this way. There is a real advantage in insulating your back and curling up. The Husky dogs sleep outdoors in 40 degrees below zero that way. You can, too, with the aid of a little fire.

EMERGENCY PACKS, ROPES AND GEAR

Rope is important. The best natural source is rolled rawhide, but there are other tying materials. The inner bark of the basswood makes excellent rope. The roots of the tamarack or the spruce provide good ties in building pack frames, canoes or bark utensils.

The black ash soaked and pounded furnishes fine withes when shaved out, from which packs and utensils can be built. Bullrushes can be used to a limited extent; and many roots have tough fibrous qualities that are useful in an emergency such as alder and birch roots. Packs can be formed of spruce frame, woven baskets, birchbark; and even pants, shirts, overalls or a tarpaulin rolled up can make pack gear.

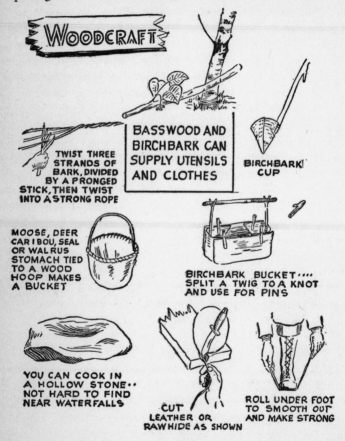

WOODCRAFT

BASSWOOD AND BIRCHBARK CAN SUPPLY UTENSILS AND CLOTHES

TWIST THREE STRANDS OF BARK, DIVIDED BY A PRONGED STICK, THEN TWIST INTO A STRONG ROPE

BIRCHBARK CUP

MOOSE, DEER CARIBOU, SEAL OR WALRUS STOMACH TIED TO A WOOD HOOP MAKES A BUCKET

BIRCHBARK BUCKET····SPLIT A TWIG TO A KNOT AND USE FOR PINS

YOU CAN COOK IN A HOLLOW STONE·· NOT HARD TO FIND NEAR WATERFALLS

CUT LEATHER OR RAWHIDE AS SHOWN

ROLL UNDER FOOT TO SMOOTH OUT AND MAKE STRONG

EMERGENCY UTENSILS

These can be made of birchbark, elm bark, rawhide; of the intestines and stomachs of larger animals; and also of the fish skins of larger fish. Hollow rocks can be heated and then soup or meat cooked by pouring in water. Extra-hot rocks can be added to continue the boiling process. Of course, when tin cans are available, your cooking gear problem is solved.

FLOATING OUT—RAFTS, BOATS AND CANOES

In much of the bush country there are many muskegs, swamps, lakes and such rugged terrain that it is difficult to walk out in cases of emergency, except in winter. Therefore, one must float out. Rafts can be built, but must be abandoned at each portage or waterfall. This method is hard. But birchbark canoes can be built, however, crude, by using some spruce framework and ribs, birchbark, pitch from balsam, spruce or red pine and spruce roots for ties. If one must travel a long distance and materials are available, constructing the bark canoe is the best measure. Where large animals are available, skins can be utilized instead of bark.

If you have large enough trees, either dugouts can be made or clapboards split out and a boat constructed. All these craft are assisted in favorable conditions of wind by sails. For example, a balsam fir, cut and stood up, makes a good sail. A rowing raft can be rigged by fastening two logs firmly about three feet apart and pointing the logs at the ends so as to cut the water. Poles about three feet high can be set in the logs for rowlocks, and sweeps (oars) can be made from spruce or ash. You can add forward and stern sweeps for negotiating rapids. Fair time is attained this way —even sail on a favorable day helps. I knew two men who sailed seventeen miles in one day on such a raft, but the craft must be strongly constructed to withstand the rigors of travel.

EMERGENCIES IN RAPIDS, WAVES AND MUSKEG BOGS

If you should be caught in a rapids, it is best not to try to stand up. Instead roll over on your back, scull your hands underneath you to keep your head as high as possible, and keep your feet downstream. This allows your feet and not your head to hit rocks. While your hands are sculling, you can reach down to push yourself off the bottom, avoiding injury. Watch your chance to steer shoreward or to get to some point of safety where your friends can rescue you. In crossing rapids on foot, you may use a long thin sapling as a brace against the current. Of course, if your party has a long rope, it is best first to send one man across with it so that he can stretch the line from the opposite bank to help the rest of the party to cross. Or if the first man is swept off his feet in his attempt to get across, the rest can haul him to safety. In crossing rapids, go slowly, make sure of the footing, each step to be well footed and braced before you take the next step. Get a line (rope) across the stream before you start over with the supplies. Don't risk duffle being carried until the way has been pioneered by the first man over and proper safeguards have been established.

A brief word should be said about waves. If possible, go with the waves. If you are swimming in heavy surf, watch the undertow, and ride the crests in to shore, especially if there are dangerous rocks. On your back, feet first, swim in on the breakers if there are any rocks or other obstructions. If you are far out, get a regular fix on the nearest point of land and work to it, for by traveling the least possible distance you have a better chance of survival. If you must swim in cold water, it is well to grease the body heavily to insulate you against the cold. Remember, keep going—don't stop —just keep plugging. If you don't, muscle cramps will set in.

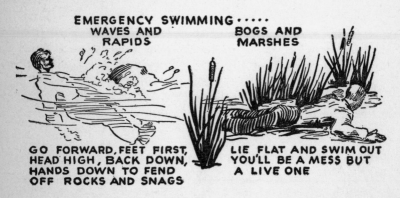

EMERGENCY SWIMMING·····
WAVES AND   BOGS AND
RAPIDS   MARSHES

GO FORWARD, FEET FIRST,   LIE FLAT AND SWIM OUT
HEAD HIGH, BACK DOWN,   YOU'LL BE A MESS BUT
HANDS DOWN TO FEND   A LIVE ONE
OFF ROCKS AND SNAGS

A real danger in cross-country travel is negotiating dangerous bogs. First of all, if you are going to cross a bog, carry a light buoyant pole. This pole is used to test the ground ahead of you for sinks. If you do get into a soupy, dangerous morass, lie flat on your stomach, keeping your feet on the surface and your face up; and using a crawl stroke and flutter kick, you can usually swim over even thick muck. Your progress will be slow, you'll be a mess when you get out, but you will survive.

WALKING OUT

If it becomes necessary to walk out of the bush, there are several things to consider: the easiest way out; the equipment to take and what to leave; and the necessity of not getting lost.

The first thing to consider is not the shortest, but the easiest way out. Often it is better to walk three times farther and avoid bad mosquito country, a rugged range of mountains or a muskeg. Maps should be studied, and careful directions and route calculations laid out after a conference with and the approval of all. After such a conference, the guide, if he is a good one, should have the final decision as his probably will be right. Once agreed, you must decide what to leave and what to take. Say, for instance, your canoes have blown away, have floated out of sight or got away down river or smashed, and you had to walk. In most wilderness areas such a circumstance presents a vital problem for all concerned. By calling a meeting of the group, you get the co-operation of all; and by having the majority with you, you obtain help in controlling those who succumb to the mental phobia, caused by fear and panic, known as "bush fever."

A word should be said about "bush fever," which is like "buck fever" (caused by excitement when trying to shoot at big game). It is a real ailment. It is a phobia, a mental set, a result of uncertainty, fear, panic, and a seemingly violent maladjustment to the strange surroundings in which the sufferer finds himself. It is a dangerous malady and a trial to everyone in the party.

I had a big six-foot four-star football player with a party, in 1927. He began to show symptoms of "bush fever." He became silent. When he talked at all, it was to say that he wanted to get out, to go home. His voice had a quaver in it. He began to get off his feed. At noon he wouldn't want to stop for lunch. He wouldn't rest but ran across the portages. He'd fuss at anyone who would stop for any reason. It wasn't long before the eight men in the party were at nerves' end. It was a rugged and dangerous country for a man to get loose in. We had a quiet conference, and I asked the co-operation of all to help keep this man from rash action. That night he refused to stop and camp because it wasn't dark yet. There was dirty muskeg country ahead, and I refused to go into it and get caught because of one member's hysteria.

We put into camp but it wasn't long before a yell from one of the men told us that the victim of bush fever had gone in an empty canoe without a pack or equipment. We grabbed the fastest canoe and by speedy paddling we caught up with him at the portage. He yelled for us to stay away and picked up a rock. I tried to talk to him, and a friend of mine who was paddling the bow maneuvered to the rear of the man and gave him a good one on the head with the broad side of the paddle. We dumped him in the canoe and hauled him back to camp. When he was revived, we called the party together, and to all assembled we laid down, in no uncertain terms, the law about staying together. He slept in my tent from then on and paddled bow in my canoe and under orders stayed with me at all times. Ten days later, as soon as we got into town where he was among familiar scenes, he became normal again. He apologized profusely, stating that he didn't know what had made him act in that way. It was nothing but the hysteria known as bush fever which is often met with in the wilderness. This "fever" is a real emergency when you run into it, and you sometimes have to take a firm hand to overcome it, as I have indicated. Every such sufferer must realize that he has to take orders for his own good and safety and for the happiness and safety of all.

To return to the subject of walking out—once a route is decided upon, then marching order should be taken. The guide leads the way, the weakest members of the party in front to set the pace, and the second in command bringing up the rear. All stay together at all times. Lay out your course. If you must detour lakes, hills, river bends, swamps or other obstructions, constantly check your compass for change in direction, time your walking of each change in direction and estimate your distance. Mark your approximate course on your map, or if you don't have a map, make one. If you don't have paper, use your handkerchief, your shirt, a piece of canvas, birchbark or a shingle of wood smoothed. Even a flat smooth rock can be used. Take bearings on outstanding landmarks, on unusual features along the trail, and snap twigs as you go in case you have to backtrack. "Hindsight" regularly. Keep your eye on the sun, wind direction, drift of the clouds and other orientation helps. If traveling on a dark day or at night, or across flat country such as spruce swamps or jackpine sand plains, a course can be steered by leaving a member to sight by compass as they can be seen or heard. Then the forward group take a "fix" ahead, etc. Three positions in a row are better than two. One other thing to remember is that it usually takes about twice as long to walk out as you originally calculated. When you're walking, especially if you're tired, a mile seems like five and you miscalculate. Two and one-half to three miles an hour with a pack through the bush is a good fast pace unless you are a professional.

SURVIVAL—HUNTING AND FISHING

To hunt and fish successfully often takes a thorough knowledge of woodcraft.

Hunting (including trapping).   This usually means stalking, catching game swimming in the water, or baiting and trapping. I have seen red squirrels and chipmunks, as well as mice, caught by placing bait in a can in which two right angle cuts across one end have formed four triangular sharp pieces of tin. These are pushed part way in. The can with the bait is placed in a tree or on ground where squirrels or chipmunks are known to be. It won't be long before they push their heads in to eat the bait, and the jagged points will hold them until you pick them up. A couple of stones in the can should give the signal for you to come and dispatch the victim. Sharp pointed wood can be used for larger game—set in a hollow log or in a woven cage or in the runs. Trigger traps can be set with sharp, fire-hardened, spearlike points on a springy strong limb. When the animal touches the bait he is speared. Figure-four deadfalls, snares, trigger traps and pits also can be used. Drawings will give you some ideas. Be sure to set your traps where you are certain the sign of animal presence is fresh and the habitat right. A little study will teach you this.

In winter muskrats can be speared through their houses, where you will also find a good supply of lily roots stored by these industrious animals. These roots, boiled with the muskrat, make a nourishing stew. It has already been explained how porcupine, grouse and ducks are caught. Moose and caribou can be killed with an axe or drowned if trapped in deep water. Bows and arrows may be fashioned of birch or black ash, clubs cut, slings made—but all of these require long practice and skill in order to master their use.

Fishing.   Fish can be taken with bone hooks and a line made of basswood bark. I know it can be done—I've done it myself several times. The most successful fish to catch are the walleyed pike, northern pike and in some places brook trout, with Grubs, minnows, crayfish, clams, or fish guts serving as bait. At night, fish can be jack-lighted by a pine torch, then speared or gigged.

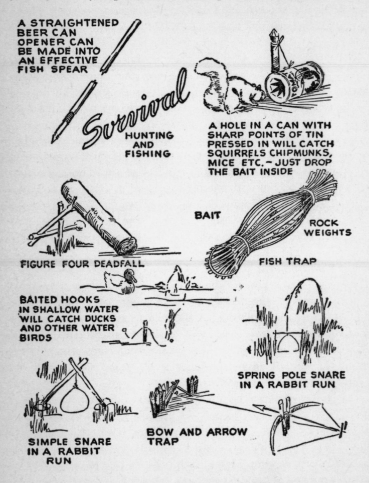

A STRAIGHTENED BEER CAN OPENER CAN BE MADE INTO AN EFFECTIVE FISH SPEAR

Survival

HUNTING AND FISHING

A HOLE IN A CAN WITH SHARP POINTS OF TIN PRESSED IN WILL CATCH SQUIRRELS CHIPMUNKS, MICE ETC. — JUST DROP THE BAIT INSIDE

BAIT

ROCK WEIGHTS

FIGURE FOUR DEADFALL

FISH TRAP

BAITED HOOKS IN SHALLOW WATER WILL CATCH DUCKS AND OTHER WATER BIRDS

SPRING POLE SNARE IN A RABBIT RUN

SIMPLE SNARE IN A RABBIT RUN

BOW AND ARROW TRAP

Fish traps, too, are quite successful, employing the principle of the aforementioned tin can. Use cage woven of alder shoots or black ash withes about three feet square, with the entrances on the sides just big enough to admit a fish and equipped with inward pointing spines to prevent the fish from getting out. Bait, such as entrails and meat, is suspended in the center. The trap is weighted by tying stones on each corner so that it will sink. Place it in the channel of a stream at a narrow part of the lake or in a likely looking hole. In the morning after an all-night set you'll have fish. Remember, this is against the law and is to be used only in survival emergencies.

WILDERNESS FIRST-AID AND CURES

Health, happiness and life depend upon your knowledge of first aid, and all trips should be provided with a first-aid kit. But if for some reason you do not have one, here are some suggestions for wilderness substitutes for some simple remedies. I will not go into the subject exhaustively, but will list only the most common emergencies and ailments which arise along the trail.

Bleeding. Bleeding can be stopped by cold applications. Or, if you are alone and can't stop the bleeding by the above method, then make use of spider webs, the dust from a puffball, a mushroom, dry powder, rotted wood from a pine, the inner bark of the hemlock or crushed calmus root—all tend to stop the flow of blood. Tourniquets are fine as a temporary measure only. Arteries must be tied off—a gut leader from your fish kit is excellent or, if necessary, ordinary string. Bind the injury with crushed green leaves or bark, such as the leaves of the sweet birch or crushed inner bark of the hemlock, since these contain iron and tannin which have a tendency to shrink small blood vessels and thus stop the bleeding. Of course, sterilized water and antiseptic must be applied to cure the wound once the emergency is past. Some old-timers even apply tobacco to a cut, the nicotine acting as an anaesthetic.

Broken Bones. These are not uncommon in wilderness travel. Any first-aid book will show the various types of splints. Only, in the wilderness, we must use the material at hand. In 1929 we brought a man out of the bush with a broken hip, injured back and broken ribs. We made him a bed in a canoe that he never left for four days. There were enough hands so that we just carried him, canoe and all, the canoe acting as a stretcher. The canoe with the patient in it was even loaded about the baggage coach, and the ambulance met us at the train when we reached home. After four days in the canoe from which the thwarts had been removed, he was finally gently lifted on a stretcher and taken to the hospital. Broken ribs are quite common and can be dangerous. The best way to handle such an injury is to pin a towel tightly around the thorax or chest—to make the patient more comfortable, hold the ribs in place and prevent splinters from puncturing the lungs. I speak with authority on the subject of broken bones, because I suffered a broken hip in 1930 and the transverse processes on the five lumbar vertebrae were broken in the spring of 1946. In each accident, it took my companions over five days to get me out of the bush.

Strained and Pulled Muscles. This perhaps is one of the most common ailments of the bush traveler. Do not be alarmed at muscle soreness as this happens even to veterans. It is caused by the unusual exertion of paddling, carrying and the other strenuous activities of trail life. First of all, take it easy at the start until all the members of the party begin to get into condition. When you are hot, do not try to cool off too fast. When you stop along the trail to rest, rub and massage leg, back and shoulder muscles. For aching or strained muscles, a soft massage at night is good remedy. It is also helpful to rub oil on yourself to keep warm. Badly strained muscles or pulled muscles should be supported by splints, bandages or a combination of both. A pulled muscle or a bad sprain can often be as troublesome and as painful as a broken bone.

Shock. Shock is recognized by cold, clammy hands and face, shallow breathing and rapid, often feeble, pulse if the victim has lapsed into unconsciousness. If he is conscious, cold sweat, clammy hands, depressed feeling, lightheadedness and rapid pulse are further signs of shock. Keep the patient warm, wrapped in blankets. If he is lying down, place his head low, give him a stimulant only if he is conscious and, above all, be reassuring. Cheer him up, make him forget what brought on the shock. Often a harrowing experience, extreme exhaustion or an injury are among the causes.

Stomach-Ache. Wild ginger tea, a hot toddy or just plain hot salt water or tea will help. Do not give laxatives as the pain may indicate more than a stomach-ache. Keep stomach warm. Wrap a hot stone in a towel, to use in the bed as a warming agent. Put patient to bed and make him comfortable.

Earache. Put some warm drops of sweet oil in the ear. Apply heat. Put patient to bed. It helps to plug the ear with cotton. If the pain continues, take a straw and blow tobacco smoke into the ear several times. This not only will stop the aching, but will often make the patient drowsy so that he will go to sleep readily.

Toothache. Sloan's Liniment, hot drops of carbolic acid or even iodine applied to cavity on cotton will give relief. Tobacco packed around it sometimes gives relief. Apply heat.

Bee Stings and Bites. Make a paste of soda bicarbonate and apply. Ammonia is also good, especially to prevent bites from itching. Mud packs seem to help, but be careful of infection.

Frostbite. Do not warm up a frostbite. If you detect it before going into a warm room, stay outside or in a cool place until treated. Rub the frozen place with snow or kerosene, or just rub until a pink glow returns to the affected areas. If it is a severe deep frostbite, see a doctor at the first possible moment. Some people prefer to thaw out frozen hands and feet by submerging in cold water and being rubbed vigorously. In the bush in winter help watch each other for the white that marks frostbite. Help each other also to keep well covered so as to prevent freezing of exposed parts.

Poison Ivy, Poison Oak or Poison Sumac. If exposed, wash immediately with strong laundry soap. Apply ferric chloride in about a 5 per cent solution. If none of this is available, the leaves of the jewelweed, clearweed or almost any tender green leaves applied will help. Dry a lather of soap on the affected spots, and this will help in some cases.

Sunburn. First, keep your shirt on. Rub face and skin with olive oil or a like substance. If a sunburn does develop, apply strong boiled tea leaves and tea, or a tea-like solution made from boiled oak bark or the inner bark of the hemlock. After application of tannic teas, apply oil or soothing ointment.

Sore Mouth. Often caused by acid foods or foods eaten too hot. Swish strong tea around in your mouth several times a day or chew the roots of the goldenthread (a small plant growing in most places and having a shiny strawberry-like leaf and golden thread-like roots).

Something in the Eye. Blow your nose hard to remove the foreign particle. If this doesn't work, locate the foreign particle and pull one eyelid down over the other. If even this doesn't work, roll the eyelid over a match or twig and remove particle with a clean handkerchief.

Emergency Rescues. Two of the most common rescues in the North country, besides the aiding of the seriously injured and the lost, involve help to those in danger of drowning when canoes upset or to the victims of ice accidents.

Upset-Canoe Rescue When a canoe upsets, don't abandon the boat. Hang on to it, it will support you. Kick and pull it to shore. If the shore is too far distant and there is another canoe with you, call or motion it to come alongside. Then, place the overturned canoe bottom-side up and at right angles amidships of the rescue canoe. When this is done, the paddlers go around and

HOLD ON TO THE CANOE AND SWIM IT TO SHORE. 1.

IF ANOTHER CANOE IS WITH YOU — PULL AT RIGHT ANGLES 2.

BOTTOM SIDE UP PULL OVER-TURNED CANOE ACROSS THE MIDDLE OF THE RESCUE CANOE 3

THE MAN IN THE WATER HELPS BY HOLDING THE OPPOSITE GUNWALE

Canoe RESCUE

4

AFTER THE WATER IS OUT—TURN RIGHT SIDE UP AND SLIDE BACK INTO THE WATER

WITH CANOES SIDE BY SIDE THE MAN IN THE WATER EASES INTO CANOE hold the opposite gunnel of the rescue canoe to give it stability. Next, the bow and sternmen in the rescue canoe pull the to-be-rescued craft bottom side up across their canoe, thus raising it up free of the water. Finally they turn it over, slide it right-side up, and steady it while those in the lake reach across amidships of their canoe and one at a time slide into it. The other canoe retrieves their paddles, and the rescue is complete. I did this kind of rescue once in the Ohio River above Louisville, Kentucky, when two men were overturned by the wake of a steamboat.

Ice Rescue To rescue a person who has fallen through ice, the rescuer must increase the area of his weight by assuming as flat a position as possible; even lying flat on his stomach if there is no other way to reach the victim. A log, branch or board extended to the victim will help. After the rescue, treat the patient for shock, and get him warm and into dry clothes as soon as possible.

Artificial Respiration Everyone who travels the bush should know how to apply artificial respiration. The patient is laid out on his stomach with his head on his flexed arm. Then, while on your knees and straddling the patient's legs, apply pressure at the base of his ribs, pressing down and forward and then snapping off. Repeat about twenty times a minute. Continue for at least an hour before giving up in case patient doesn't revive.

SUMMARY

As a summary, let us say in any accident keep cool and calm. Survey the situation. Be sure that the patient has no broken bones before moving and stop all bleeding at once. Then apply first aid, keeping everything sterile and putting antiseptic on all wounds. If serious, get patient to a doctor at once. As a final word, try to foresee danger. Avoid it! Avoid taking unnecessary risks. You'll have enough adventure without looking for trouble.

SUPPLEMENT TO CHAPTER

LIVING OFF THE LAND (*Using nature's storehouse to supplement your grub for survival*)

MEAT AND ANIMAL PRODUCTS

Game. (Use only according to law unless in dire emergency.) Moose, caribou, deer, bears, seals, rabbits, mice, squirrels, chipmunks, lemmings, porcupines, marmots, muskrats, beaver. (Where found.)

Birds. Ducks, geese, ruffed grouse, sharp-tailed grouse, spruce grouse, Franklin grouse, ptarmigan. You can eat anything that flies; in case of emergency, even gulls and loons, the world's worst eating.

Eggs. Birds' eggs in season can be eaten, also turtle eggs, where found.

Shortening. Fat of bear, geese, ducks, porcupine, moose, deer, caribou can be rendered, used and carried in stomach skins or birchbark buckets. (Indians in early days used to make butter of fat passenger pigeons.)

Greases and other oils. Practically all fish give off oils upon rendering. These are good for leather dressing, lamp oil. Seals, walrus and other marine mammals, such as porpoise, are a rich source of oils and fats. Fish oils and fats usually are not used in cooking because of the taste, but they are valuable.

Fish and aquatic foods. Fish, frogs, turtles, clams, water snails, salamanders—all are an important source of food and can be eaten. Snakes also can be eaten. I have eaten them, and they are good roasted, baked or fried. Even grubs make good tasty food if you are starving.

VEGETABLES (*substitutes*)

Potatoes. Root of ten-petaled sun flower, cattail roots, root and root shoots of water lily, root and root shoots of great green bullrush. Root of skunk cabbage and jack-in-the-pulpit, boiled several times to remove the taste. Root of Canadian Solomon seal, Indian cucumber. Arrowhead lily, golden club, Jerusalem artichoke also can be used.

Beans and Green Beans. Buds of basswood, new balsam tips, brake fern, fiddleheads in early spring, tick trefoil, vetch and black pea.

Onions. Wild leek, wild onions, garlic, where found.

Spinach and Greens. Lamb's quarter, wild lettuce, dandelion, sorrel, plantain, sour dock, chickweeds, purslane, mustard, spring beauty.

Peas. Vetch seeds, black peas, tick trefoil.

Salad Vegetables. Indian cucumber roots, spring beauty roots, sorrel, oxalis, young dandelion, wild lettuce, lamb's quarter, watercress, root stems of green bullrush.

Mushrooms. Many varieties can be eaten. Be sure they are not one of the deadly Anametias. If they grow on rotted wood, you are safe.

CEREALS

Wild rice where available. There are many glutens that can be substituted for flour—dock seed ground, hazelnuts ground, and bulbs of water lily, bullrush and cattail boiled till soft, ground up and dried and pulverized. Buds of basswood boiled and treated in the same way make gluten. Lichens such as the rock tripe give off gluten if boiled and strained. Any starchy root can be boiled and gluten can be obtained to add starch to the diet.

FRUITS

Fruits are abundant throughout the North country in season. Some can even be found dry in winter. Blueberries, high-bush cranberries, strawberries, cranberries, service or June berries, blackberries, red raspberries, and fruit of the ground hemlock. Many of these can be dried whole and preserved.

NUTS

Nuts are not too common in the wilderness. However, the hazelnut, although small compared with southern varieties, can still be gathered and used in season. The roots of the spring beauty (Claytonia virginica) can be boiled, and they taste like chestnuts. In the southern part of Canada some oaks are found, and the bitterness can be boiled out of acorns to make them eatable. In fact, ground up, they make good bread.

TEA, COFFEE AND OTHER BEVERAGES

Tea substitutes can be made from the flowers of basswood, young fresh tips of willow in spring, as well as from young birch shoots, spruce, balsam and hemlock tips. Fragrant teas can be made from any of the mints, spice bush, sweet anise, wild sarsaparilla, sweet birch twigs and bergamot.

Coffee substitutes may be roasted and charred grains, hazelnuts, dandelion and lettuce roots and, of course, chicory root where found.

Wild fruit juices—from the cranberry, blueberry, strawberry, service berry—all make delicious and refreshing drinks. Spruce and hemlock young shoots also make a delicious drink.

Cocoa substitute: young basswood fruit mashed gives the flavor of chocolate.

SUGAR

Sap of maple and beech, boiled down. Wild honey. And sugar obtained from such wild fruits as the service berry, which is high in sugar content.

FLAVORING

All the following make good flavorings: for onion—wild leek; pepper—pepper grass; mustard—wild mustard; horseradish—grated Indian turnip mixed with Indian cucumber and vinegar; and mints, sarsaparilla, sweet anise, and spicewood. Pepper can also be made from powdered, dried root of Indian turnip charred a little.

chapter 9

WILDERNESS SPORT

The great wilderness areas of our continent and the world, and their resources, are faced with the serious problems posed by the airplane, the automobile, the repeating rifle and modernized fishing equipment. It is with a sigh of relief that some of us old-timers have watched the growth of the science of conservation, the science of protecting and increasing our wildlife, fish and animal, and our forest preserves. Areas once threatened with extermination of man's greatest heritage, the out-of-doors and its sport, have now been developed by scientific supervision to a point where fish and game are more plentiful by far than they were in the days of the pioneer. The great game preserves of Africa, Canada, Western United States, Minnesota, Wisconsin, Michigan, Pennsylvania, New York, and many other areas show clearly that game and fish management is one of the very important forward movements of our time. Development of recreation through the conservation of our natural resources of water, forest, sand and the natural wild inhabitants therein is a project that should be backed to the hilt by all of us. Fish experts now battle to eliminate such harmful fish as the lamprey, the dogfish and others. In addition, they have promoted the science of fish hatching and planting to such an extent that in many places care has to be taken not to overpopulate our streams and lakes. In fact in many sections, especially in the United States, there is actually the serious problem of the over-population of fish.

Game is also being developed with careful handling so that the woods traveler has the joy of seeing wild animals in their natural state and an opportunity to hunt them in season. We are finding that these factors are a stabilizing influence in our modern civiliza-tion. If mankind would, on occasion, revert to primitive living, re-turn to nature and follow basic instincts to hunt and fish, we should be a more stabilized race. If we are able to maintain a homespun and solid basic philosophy of living, which can only be derived from our original and native environment, namely the wild country, we shall survive emotionally the great human emer-gencies which the world faces periodically.

The subject of hunting and fishing is so extensive that this sec-tion of the book will be devoted primarily to equipment for these sports. There will also be a brief listing of the game fish, birds and animals available in the wild areas of our continent.

FISHING EQUIPMENT

The problem of carrying fishing tackle on the trail is a major one. It often costs a man (or woman) a hundred dollars a fish be-cause upon arrival at a selected and remote fishing spot, he finds his tackle broken or inadequate. This is a real loss, especially if the trip was taken primarily to catch fish. All equipment should be packed in compact strong containers. The rods and rod cases should be lashed under the gunnels of the canoe; plugs and hooks of all kinds should be kept in puncture-proof containers except when in active use. The details of proper packing of both fishing and hunting equipment should be carefully worked out before you take a trip. Another thing to keep in mind is to have plenty of what you need for fishing, but also eliminate the useless and un-used stuff that practically every fisherman carries around with him. This will take some diplomacy, but it can be done.

I remember distinctly one chap who wanted to take three cast-ing rods and six reels with him. He also had over fifty varieties of plugs in a large steel box that weighed as much as two weeks' rations. We finally got him down to two casting rods, two reels and lines, and a two-and-a-half-pound pressed-top can in which we carried five floating plugs and ten trolling baits with some extra hooks, leaders, swivels and sinkers. Instead of weighing the original forty pounds, it now weighed about six pounds. Later, after a rough mountain portage, he saw the light, and because he was such a good sport, we went out of our way to see that he landed some prize fish, including a thirty-eight-pound lake trout and a four-and-a-half-pound speckled trout.

The following is a good all-round fishing outfit that can be used on a trip into the wilderness if fishing is your objective. There is only one change. If you are in the Eastern Maritime Provinces of Canada and going after Atlantic salmon, you carry a heavier salmon rod instead of the standard 4-to-6-ounce fly rod used on speckled trout.

Fly-Fishing Outfit:

1. Six-ounce standard make split bamboo fly casting rod, with extra tip, and reel. Always have a good rod case that cannot be easily bent or broken.

2. One rod repair kit, small long-nosed pliers with short cut, wrapping silk, extra leads, extra ferrules, and tips, ferrule glue and small bottle of quick-drying varnish.

3. Book of wet and dry flies. Keep to the neutral colors for trout dry flies, such as grays, browns, black, etc. These are the cahills, algomas, coachman, black gnats, adams, great dun, march brown, etc. Sizes #10 to #16 hook will be desirable to give variety. In choosing wet flies, remember that often you are trying to imitate a minnow; consequently, take such streamer flies as the parmachene belle. Reds and whites are good for bass and also landlocked salmon. The smaller wet flies seem to work better for speckled trout. In all cases of wet flies, a tiny Colorado spinner attached helps a great deal.

4. A series of small spinners, swivels and fasteners—some extra small-sized long-shanked hooks for live-bait casting with a fly rod.

5. Your fishing coat also should contain extra gut leaders, a leader soaking case, line dressing, mucelin, some paraffined matches,

a pair of finger nippers for trimming gut leader and flies, and a good pocket knife for cleaning fish.

6. Other equipment would be a landing net and, if you are advised that you can wade the streams (not possible in many parts of Canada or Western United States), take a creel and either hip boots or scotch waders. *It is good to take a tape measure just for the record.*

Bait-Casting Outfit:

If there is a choice between a fly-casting and a bait-casting outfit, and yours is to be a long trip, take your bait-casting outfit. With it, you can catch a greater variety of fish.

Small light-metal tackle box with rounded corners and tools for reel repair. Take for all-around fishing not too many, but enough, assorted spoons, daredevils, etc. Spinners, large and small, from large buck tail spinners on. Tiny Colorado spinners are excellent for trout. Plugs—redhead floating and sinking, jitterbugs, riverrunts, and the like. Bass seem to like red and white bait. Pike take anything. Walleyes like deep spinners such as the Shannon spinner.

Weedless underwater trolling bait—there are many kinds which often catch bass when they won't rise to a plug. The Hawaiian wiggler is a good one. Assorted hooks ranging from small bluegill hooks and fine hooks (for catching shiners and chubs for bait) to the large ones with a two-and-one-half-inch shank. Wire and gut leaders—snaps and swivels, assorted sinkers, split shot of varying sizes work well. Tools—small pair of short-cut long-nose pliers, two or three sizes of small screw drivers, small roll of light copper wire, length of solder wire carrying own acid, small strong bottle of varnish and small brush. Small can of reel oil; extra line (silk braided), extra leads (line guides), collapsible landing net, small-jointed gaff hook, net live keep, short-joint tubular casting rod, preferably agate guides, reel and reel case.

The weight of the above outfit should be kept down—not more than from four to seven pounds in all. It should be compact so that it will all fit in a packsack. When the camper is not portaging too much, steel rods can be tied inside under the gunwales of the canoe.

Trolling Rig:

Short heavy trolling pole and reel can be carried for deep trolling with from three hundred to five hundred feet of woven copper line. Spoons, spinners can be used. Archer spinner is a good one for lake trout.

FISHING

Below are listed some of the outstanding game fish and where they can be found in the United States and Canada. (Some species have several names.)

FISH	LOCATION	BAIT NEEDED
Atlantic Salmon	Eastern Maritime Provinces of New Brunswick, Quebec, Prince Edward Island, Nova Scotia, Newfoundland, Labrador.	Dry and wet flies of choice advised.
Speckled Trout	Very generally distributed, but mostly east of the Continental Divide in natural state. Not associated pike waters; heterogeneous in distribution. Not found in muddy streams but in streams where sand and rocks predominate as trout cannot stand sediment. Usually occur in swiftwater streams or deep cold-water lakes. Found in almost every state in the Union and Province in Canada.	Wet and dry flies of choice or those advised by local fishermen; minnows and worms; spinners; grubs; crickets; grasshoppers, etc.

FISH	LOCATION	BAIT NEEDED
Landlocked Salmon (Ouananiche)	Inland in Maine, Eastern Maritime Provinces of Canada and into eastern Ontario very locally. I know of only one lake adjacent to Lake Superior that has landlocked salmon.	Spinners and minnows with long- and short-hook combination; wet and dry flies at certain times of the year.
Lake Trout (Several Varieties)	Widely distributed; found primarily in lakes west into British Columbia from Atlantic Coast and far into the north. Found in Minnesota, Wisconsin, Michigan, New York and New England.	Trolling baits; silver spoons of many varieties; Archer spinner is excellent; caught with shiners and chubs as live bait.
Rainbow Trout or Steelhead (Western Steelhead is practically the same)	Lake Superior and Lake Huron and local in adjacent streams. Also found in Alberta, British Columbia, Northwestern and Western United States, and planted in other parts of the United States.	Dry and wet flies; squirrel tail wet fly is excellent; minnows, small spinners and spoons; sometimes have been caught with worms.
German Brown Trout	Planted trout in trout areas in more populated and fished regions.	Same flies and bait as speckled trout.
Smallmouthed Black Bass	Heterogeneously distributed, primarily following the Great	Bait casting with plugs, spoons, and spinners; live bait

FISH	LOCATION	BAIT NEEDED
	Lakes and St. Lawrence drainage. They are found in both lakes and rivers, practically throughout the entire United States.	of minnows, soft craws, frogs, crickets and grasshoppers; grubs and worms at certain seasons; also taken on wet flies, poppers and occasionally dry flies.
Largemouthed Black Bass	Same as smallmouthed bass, but more southern in distribution; usually found in weed-bearing lakes.	Same bait as smallmouth bass.
Walleyed Pike (Pickerel)	Wide distribution east of Rockies in lakes and larger rivers; however, found mostly in the northern states and throughout Canada.	Spinners, spoons, daredevils especially effective; minnows caught usually deep not rising to surface as bass or trout.
Northern Pike	Wide distribution throughout Canada east of the Rockies and northern United States.	Plugs, spinners, spoons, large minnows. They bite at almost anything.
Muskalunge or Muskinange (spelled in several other ways.)	In Great Lakes (except Lake Erie) and their drainages from Rainey River, Kenora and Lake of the Woods District, etc. Minnesota and Wisconsin are famous for "musky" fishing.	Large minnows; large spoons; large spinners; large buck-tail spinners.

FISH	LOCATION	BAIT NEEDED
Bluegills, Long-eared Sunfish, Green Sunfish, other Sun Perch species	Southern Canadian waters west to Saskatchewan, and practically in all parts of the United States.	Minnow, worms, small spinners; dry fly, wet fly, poppers, etc.
Arctic Char (also called Sea Salmon or Trout)	Yukon, Northwest Territory; northwest tip of Quebec in Ungava; Labrador.	Spearing by Indians; spinners, spoons, dry and wet flies.
Arctic Grayling	Widely distributed in Far North.	Minnows, spinners, spoons, etc.
Grayling (natives call them Sailor Trout)	Getting rare in Ontario or Quebec. Still found in isolated lakes. Also found in Alberta and British Columbia. Not found in United States except in a few isolated areas.	Dry flies, wet flies; small spinners; minnows and live bait.
Kamloops Trout	British Columbia	Dry fly; wet fly; spinner; minnows; worms.
Dolly Varden	Alberta, Yukon, British Columbia.	Same as above.
Cutthroat Trout	Alberta, British Columbia	Same as above.
Pacific Salmon (Several Species)	Coastal streams of British Columbia.	Spoons, spinners, large minnows.

It should be noted that the interior of British Columbia, the Yukon, Northwest Territory, northern (Arctic) Quebec and Labrador still contain game fish, especially of the trout and salmon families, still to be classified by scientists.

A word should be said about commercial and food fish. The

whitefish, the herring, perch, chubs, and many other excellent food fish are found in quantities all over the North country. The gold eye, the smelt, the ling, the sturgeon and many others are an important story in themselves. The rivers of the United States, such as the Ohio, Mississippi, etc., present a variety of semicommercial fish some of which are good sport to catch—as the catfish.

To the reader I apologize for this sketchy handling of a big subject. Fishing brings so much pleasure to so many persons that it was felt that more space should have been given to it.

> For mighty streams and quiet hills,
> For the thousand days of fisherman's thrills
> For lands that far o'er the horizon's rim,
> Back in the Bush where the trail is dim,
> For balm from life's long cares and woes,
> For places of beauty where the fisherman goes,
> Thank you, Lord, for rest from care.
> I've tasted paradise out there!

HUNTING EQUIPMENT

The proper equipment for hunting varies with your quarry. If it is geese and ducks, a shotgun and heavy shot are used (up to #4. Or if it is deer, a shotgun with slugs or buckshot may be used. But if you are going after bear, moose or mountain sheep, it is an entirely different problem. There are several things to keep in mind if your hunt is for big game. In general, carry an all-purpose gun such as a .30-06 or a .30-30 or .32 Special. However, for specific hunting of such game as sheep, which is always a long-range sport, a .270 or .308 Winchester, a .30/06 or .300 H & H Magnum with scopes and accurate adjustments are necessary for success. The gun to carry for general wilderness travel if you are hunting is 20 gauge in shotguns; or a carbine, Winchester, Remington or any other standard make with .30-30 or .32 speecial caliber. A short gun is preferable for general use as is a shotgun that can be broken down, since the proper place to carry a gun (except on the hunt) is in a case packed into your packsack. Big guns and long rifles become a problem if they are carried on horseback, in the dog sled, in a canoe or just in packing on the trail. Be sure to carry enough ammunition, but not enough to fight a war. For big game, 20 or

25 shells is plenty; and for birds it will take considerably more, according to the amount of shooting you expect to do.

Equipment for hunting, and care of your gun:

1. Gun (whatever kind you will need and carry).
2. Cleaning materials, rod, patches, wiping rags, oil, nitro-solvent and gun grease for protecting metal surfaces against weather.
3. Gun Case—leather is the best. Carry small can of Neat's-foot oil to keep case in shape.
4. Ammunition containers, preferably leather or canvas. Shotgun ammunition should also be rolled into a water- and moisture-proof cover.
5. Repair kit—long-nosed pliers, several sizes of screw-drivers, steel wool, punch, small file and needed extra spare parts.
6. Extra attachments such as scopes, sights, etc., according to what is being hunted.
7. A sling is always good equipment for guns on the trail even for carbines and shotguns.

HUNTING

Hunting can be divided into two categories. First, game bird hunting and, second, general game hunting including big game. I will treat the two only briefly since each alone could fill a large volume.

Bird Hunting—Water, Marsh and Upland. Most water birds are classified as migratory, including the ducks, geese, coots and others. These flock down in the autumn over four main flyways—the Atlantic and Pacific coasts, the central main flyways of Hudson Bay down over the Great Lakes to the Gulf of Mexico, the great lake Winnipeg and the Mississippi Valley flyway. The hunting months are from September to January, according to your geographical location. The universal gun is the shotgun with heavy load shells varying from #4 goose shot to #8½ bird shot. There are many ways of bringing down ducks and geese, dependent on the country you find yourself in and its game laws.

Marsh and upland hunting is a category in itself, and fine skill is required to stalk the wily woodcock, rail, quail or grouse with gun and dog. For upland birds usually #6 to #8½ shots are used with heavier load and #4 and #5 shots for wild turkey. The best advice I can give you on bird hunting, because of the fact that there is such a wide variance in opinion, is to obtain the advice of your guide, the local inhabitants and the local outfitter as to the best methods in the region of hunting the type of bird you are seeking. After more than a quarter of century of bird hunting in many places, from the subtropics to the Arctic, and after shooting many kinds of feathered game, I firmly believe the above recommendation is best. Then, too, if I tried to present this information, I would require a huge volume to cover the subject.

I definitely believe, however, that the laws of your hunting locality should be rigidly observed. In addition, take only the amount of game you need so that those who come after you will share too the joys that you are experiencing now.

Below are listed most of the game birds of our continent.

LIST OF GAME BIRDS OF CANADA AND THE UNITED STATES

NAME	OCCURRENCE	DISTRIBUTION
Ducks:		
Mallard	Common	General
Black Duck	Common	Central-Eastern
Gadwall	Fairly common	Western-Central, sometimes Eastern
European Widgeon	Uncommon	Eastern
Baldpate	Common	General
Green-winged Teal	Common	General
Blue-winged Teal	Common	General
Cinnamon Teal	Rare	Western
Shoveler	Common	General
Pin Tail	Common	General
Wood duck	Uncommon	Southern Canada
Red Head	Fairly common	General
Canvasback	Not common	General
Scaup	Fairly common	General
Lesser Scaup	Common	Southern Canada
Ring Neck Duck	Not common	General
Golden Eye	Not common	General

NAME	OCCURRENCE	DISTRIBUTION
Ducks (cont.)		
Barrows Golden Eye	Not common	General
Bufflehead	Fairly common	General
Old Squaw	Fairly common (Sea Duck)	General, mostly along coast
Harlequin	Not common	General, mostly along coast
Eider	Rare	Eastern
Scoter	Uncommon	General, Northern
White-winged Scoter	Uncommon	General, but mostly coastal
Surf Scoter	Uncommon	Coastal waters
Ruddy Duck	Uncommon	General
American Merganser	Common	General
Red-breasted Merganser	Common	General
Hooded Merganser	Fairly common	General
Geese:		
Canada Goose	Common	General
Blue Goose	Fairly common	Eastern
Snow Goose	Fairly common	Western; Central-Eastern—rare
White-fronted Goose	Uncommon	Western-Central East—rare
Brant	Uncommon	Eastern coast occasionally Central
Black Brant	Uncommon	Western coast
Emperor Goose	Rare	Western coast
Whistling Swan	Uncommon—protected	General
Trumpeter Swan	Rare—protected	Western
Marsh Birds:		
King Rail	Rare (should be protected)	Eastern
Virginia Rail	Common, but not abundant	Central-Eastern

NAME	OCCURRENCE	DISTRIBUTION
Marsh Birds (cont.)		
Sora Rail	Common, but not abundant	General
Gallinules	Not common in Canada	Not common
Coot	Common	General
Wilson Snipe	Not common	General
Woodcock	Fairly common	Eastern-Central
Upland Game Birds:		
Quail	Common	U.S. East of Great Plain
Ruffed Grouse	Common	Eastern and North Central
Spruce Grouse	Common, though often local	Rockies, east to Labrador (in forests) of Canada
Franklin Grouse	Not common	Western Canada
Willow Ptarmigan	Common	Far North— Western
Rock Ptarmigan	Common	Far North—Yukon
White-tailed Ptarmigan	Uncommon	Western Canada
Prairie Chicken	Common locally	Central Canada and northern U.S.
Sharp-tailed Grouse	Fairly common	General
Sage Hen	Uncommon	Western
Pheasants	Local	Southern Ontario— Manitoba and northern U.S.
Mourning Dove	Common	General in eastern U.S.
Wild Turkey	Local distributed	Southern (two-thirds) of U.S. in wild country
California Quail	Common	Southwest U.S.

Four-Legged Game Hunting. The subject of hunting various wild game in North America is extensive and varied and would fill volumes. It is best to learn about the local methods of hunting various game from the fire and game wardens, professional hunters, or your guide and outfitter. Inquire directly from these people whether you are to stalk caribou by getting down wind from them and waiting for them to drift toward you across the tundre, as is characteristic of the movements of caribou; or whether you are to sit among the rocks to wait for the mountain sheep to come into an alpine meadow, as they are accustomed to do in order to take a siesta in the afternoon sunshine; or whether you are to sit by a deer run in Michigan or work and stalk a ridge for mule or black-tailed deer in the West, or just give a shrill whistle to freeze a woodchuck in the cross-hairs of your scope.

A word of safety and caution in regard to big and dangerous game: always go along with experienced and well-recommended guides. Be well informed where, how and when to shoot. Carry proper gun and ammunition, suited to the game you are hunting. For instance, it is suicide to hunt polar bear by small boat, canoe or kayak. A polar bear knows no fear; he is very hard to kill, and no man or small boat is a match for him for speed and power in the water. You shoot between his eyes and the bullet will glance off as it will off a grizzly bear or a brownie. Even when they have been shot through the heart, I have seen bears run almost a half a mile. Many a bear thus wounded has mauled a hunter and often killed him before the beast died. Break the neck—by shooting behind the ear or under the chin center—as any experienced big-game hunter will tell you about the bear, our most dangerous big game.

Moose, caribou and deer present a different problem in stalking and shooting. Many a hunter will sit all day as he would for a deer when hunting moose and wonder why he didn't see or get a shot. He should have a guide show him how to cast about for signs of the moose's browsing on birch twigs or willows and proceed to track and stalk the moose. Even the common cottontail rabbit presents a problem all its own and varies in its habits from the snowshoe rabbit. Thus each animal becomes a fascinating study. Since this is a book about wilderness travel and not about hunting, a list of North American big game, methods of stalking it, and the best guns to use will be given below. It is hoped that this table will help you to better hunting on your next wilderness trip.

CANADIAN GAME ANIMALS—LARGE AND SMALL

NAME	DISTRIBUTION, HABITAT	METHOD OF HUNTING	BEST GUN OR IMPLEMENT TO USE
DEER FAMILY—(*Cervidae*)			
White-tailed or Virginia Deer	Southern Canada in forests east to west	Still hunting (sitting, driving)	Buckshot, 30-30, 30/06, 32 Sp., 35 Win., 303 Sav., 348 Win.
Mule Deer	Western Canada; forests, hilly country to semi-open country	Stalking along ridges, still hunting, driving	Need longer-range rifle, often 348 Win., 270 Win., 30/06, 7 M.M. Mauser
Black-tailed Deer	Far West and Southern; forest, mountains and hilly country	Stalking along ridges, still hunting, driving	Same guns as for mule deer
Elk	Western Canada, mountains, forested hills	Stalking, driving and tracking	270 Win., 348 Win., 303 Sav., 30/06, 30/40, 7.9 Mauser
Moose	Canada in general distribution in forest areas	Stalking, trailing and watching feeding areas, use of calling horn	Same gun as for elk
Woodland Caribou	Northern woodland areas from New-	Stalking, tracking, watching	Long-range gun often

NAME	DISTRIBUTION, HABITAT	METHOD OF HUNTING	BEST GUN OR IMPLEMENT TO USE
	foundland to British Columbia, but local	river crossing, using wind-drift habit for stalking and snow camouflage helps	with scope, 30/06, 270 Win., 7.9 Mauser, 300 H. & H. Magnum, 348 Win.
Newfoundland Caribou	Newfoundland	Same	Same
Barren Ground Caribou	Barren grounds, general northern Canada	Same	Same
Stone Caribou	West of McKenzie River, Northwest Territories, Yukon	Same	Same
Reindeer	Yukon, Northwest Territories introduced	Protected	Protected

OTHER HOOFED GAME OF CANADA—*(Bovidae)*—(Oxen, Sheep and Goats)

Antelope	Alberta	Protected	
Musk Ox	Far North, mostly north of Arctic Circle	Protected	
Rocky Mountain Sheep	Western mountains from U.S. border to Arctic	Stalking from above if possible, using field glasses, white camouflage good in snow	High powered scope rifles, as 308 Win., 30/06, 300 H. & H. Magnum, 270 Win.
Dall Mountain Sheep	Subarctic in Yukon and northern British Columbia	Same	Same
Faunin Mountain Sheep	Similar to Dall Mountain Sheep	Same	Same

NAME	DISTRIBUTION, HABITAT	METHOD OF HUNTING	BEST GUN OR IMPLEMENT TO USE
Stone Mountain Sheep	Northern Alberta and British Columbia and Yukon	Same	Same
Rocky Mountain Goat	British Columbia and Yukon (southern)	Same	Same
Columbia Rocky Mountain Goat	Same	Same	Same
Buffalo	Alberta	Protected	

BEARS OF CANADA—(Ursidae)

NAME	DISTRIBUTION, HABITAT	METHOD OF HUNTING	BEST GUN OR IMPLEMENT TO USE
Black Bear	All forested areas of lower Canada, including brown phases of Western Canada	Still hunting near feeding places, tracking, driving	30-30, 30/06, 35 Win., 30 Sav., 348 Win., 270 Win., 303 British
Polar Bear	Arctic waters and Hudson Bay, sometimes James Bay	Hunted by boat or stalked along shore ice	Use heavy impact gun, 300 H. & H. Magnum, 405, 375 Magnum
Grizzly Bear	Western mountains and foothills up to Arctic Circle	Hunting best in spring or late fall. Found on spring slides, berry patches. Stalking or tracking	Same
Barren Ground Bear	Barren grounds between McKenzie River and Hudson Bay (very rare)	Stalking or tracking	Same

NAME	DISTRIBUTION, HABITAT	METHOD OF HUNTING	BEST GUN OR IMPLEMENT TO USE
	CATS OF CANADA—*(Felidae)*		
Mountain Lion Cougar	British Columbia north to about 60° parallel	Hounds; tracking, trapping. Some have been caught in mating season.	30-30, 30/06, 32 Sp., 348 Win., 300 and 303 Sav., 248 Win., 270 Win.
Lynx	East to west in forested areas, usually above	Tracking; dogs; or trapping	Shot gun, #2 or #3 shot or light rifle
Wild Cat	Forested areas of lower Canada, east to west	Same	Same
	RABBITS OF CANADA AND THE UNITED STATES—*(Leporidae)*		
Cottontail or Grey Rabbit	Southern Canada, mostly eastern and eastern U.S.	Tracking; general hunting; hounds, and driving	Shotgun, 12, 16 or 20, 410 gauge. Light rifle as 22 caliber
Jack Rabbit	Alberta, Saskatchewan, Manitoba (southern) in open country and western U.S.	Dogs; tracking, general hunting and driving	Same
Arctic Hare	Arctic and barren lands	Tracking, driving	Same
Varying Hare or Snowshoe Rabbit	Many variations but general throughout forested areas of Canada	Dogs; tracking, driving or general hunting	Same
	RACCOON—*(Procyonidae)*		
Raccoon	Lower eastern Canada and eastern U.S.	Night hunting with hounds, trapping	Small-calibered rifle or shotgun

NAME	DISTRIBUTION, HABITAT	METHOD OF HUNTING	BEST GUN OR IMPLEMENT TO USE
	FOXES, WOLVES OF CANADA—(*Canidae*)		
Timber or Grey wolf	General over Canada, usually in forested areas—some parts of U.S.	Tracking, baiting; very difficult to hunt; trapping	30-30, 32 Sp., 35 Win., shotgun with buck-shot
Arctic or White Wolf	Arctic—questionable	This is almost legendary—some question as to existence	Same
Coyote	Canadian plains region, Alberta, Saskatchewan and Manitoba. Also Mich., Wis. and western U.S.	Dogs, horse, car; tracking, baiting, trapping	Same, except scope used for long range
Red Fox	Wide range in Canada; more prevalent in central, east and northeast and U.S. general	Dogs, tracking, baiting, trapping	Shotgun, light rifle
Cross Fox	Variation of Red Fox. Canada	Same	Same
Black Fox	Rare but same as above, variation of Red Fox	Same	Same
Silver Fox	Same as above	Same	Same
Prairie, Kit or Swift Fox	Prairies, principally Saskatchewan and western U.S.	Same	Same
Arctic or White Fox	Several variations, Arctic regions	Tracking, baiting and trapping	Same
Blue Fox	Variation of White Fox	Same	Same

NAME	DISTRIBUTION, HABITAT	METHOD OF HUNTING	BEST GUN OR IMPLEMENT TO USE

Weasel Family—(*Mustelidae*)
(Being nocturnal in habit, the weasels are trapped)

NAME	DISTRIBUTION, HABITAT	METHOD OF HUNTING	BEST GUN OR IMPLEMENT TO USE
American Wolverine	Wide distribution in forested areas of Canada, rare in east and central, rather common in northwest	Very difficult to trap	Trap
Fisher or Pennant Martin	Not common, but found in general over Canada in heavy forests	Trapping	Trap
American Martin	Not common, has several variations, found in dense forests	Trapping— baiting	Trap
Arctic Weasel or Ermine	Arctic general	Trapping	Trap
Weasel	Many variations, widely distributed	Trapping	Trap
Mink	General distribution especially in forest areas, usually near lakes or streams	Trapping	Trap
Otter	General distribution, several variations	Trapping	Trap
Skunk	Lower eastern Canada, all parts of the Eastern and Central and Southern U.S.	Trapping; in some cases dogs used	Traps and light calibered rifle
Badger	Ontario, local; Manitoba, southern and Saskatchewan and western U.S.	Trapping	Trap

NAME	DISTRIBUTION, HABITAT	METHOD OF HUNTING	BEST GUN OR IMPLEMENT TO USE
GNAWING GAME ANIMALS—*(Rodentia)*			
Woodchuck	Lower Ontario, northern, eastern and southern U.S.	Watching the feeding grounds	High-speed light-calibered scope rifle
Marmot	Several sub-species; Western Canada north to barren grounds and western U.S.	Same	Same
Beaver	Canada, generally in forested areas and northern, western U.S.	Trapped in runways and houses	Trap
Porcupine	Eastern and central Canada in forested areas and northern U.S.	Emergency food obtained with a club	Not usually molested
Muskrat	General east and central Canada and U.S.	Trapped in houses or runways	Trap

NEW HORIZONS

In the hurry and stress and often nerve-racking bustle of our modern civilization, it is sometimes hard to keep a sound and uncluttered point of view. Underneath the surface, most of us quietly yearn for far away places and a simpler life. This urge, basic and real, looks for relief from the tensions of our daily tasks, our home responsibilities and the worrying headlines of the newspapers. The greatest luxury for many of us is just to have the opportunity to be quietly alone with ourselves and our thoughts and to have a chance to shake off the blatant civilization that we live in. One of the best cures that I have found for all these tensions is to sit back, close my eyes, and dream of a thousand campfires, the majesty of blue hills, lakes and winding calm rivers with new vistas of beauty around each bend; perhaps of quiet moonlight nights and the little music of a bird singing in his sleep, or the long call of an old dog wolf looking at the moon and talking to his kin somewhere out in the vastness of the night. Perhaps it is a dream of good companions and high adventure on some hunt or of a group around the fire studying a tattered blueprint map in order to plan the trail for the next day. Or I may be carried in thought to some high mountain to sit, lost in reverie, with a gun on my lap and watch a sun-drenched alpine meadow below with the backdrop of distant purple mountain peaks.

When life gets complicated, scrape together your funds and go on a wilderness trip. It is a good investment in restoring your soul, your point of view, your physical and mental health; and it will add to your store of memories when, back in civilization, you wish to recall fond experiences while smoking your pipe and relaxing. If you have never followed the open trail, try it. It is not hard, it is fun. And whether you are new or old at the game, it will add never-ending pleasure and health and new horizons to your living. In closing this book, I beg your indulgence while I give a personal example of how a wilderness trip can originate.

The phone jangled all day. My secretary, busy close by, was in one of her "off-day moods" and peeled my hide off with a withering look every time I motioned toward a pile of week-old correspondence and other things that had to be done. Everyone who came to my desk brought a peck of trouble, overdue reports stared me in the face, and I received a request to attend a meeting and eat food about which I had no choice. In a moment of desperation I pulled out the center desk drawer for a pipe with a well-chewed bit, caused by just such occasions, and discovered the last straw—I had left it at home. Despondent, I pulled the drawer out further to look in its little-seen back corners, and there to my delight I found an old briar pipe, long forgotten among the rubble of articles put there because they were too valuable to be thrown away but which were never used. I pulled it out and along with it an old buckskin zippered pouch in which was enough Hudson Bay Imperial Mixture to plug the battered bowl. Quietly sliding the drawer closed and keeping a wary eye on "her majesty" whacking away on a supposedly noiseless typewriter, I lighted up with a "horse match" and, after a puff or two, leaned back and relaxed.

Toying with the old pipe, I seemed to feel at last as if an understanding friend was close. It was broken, a thin strip of babiche rawhide holding the fractured stem together and plugging up the leaks in the old pipe. How well I remember the day I broke it. . . .

It had been a long, rough trip of more than a hundred portages, and with some three hundred miles of water behind us. We were traveling down on the Lake Superior drainage from away over the Hudson Bay Divide. Our portage just then was Shaking

Mountain on the Montreal River, and only recently we had passed over the dangerous Golden Stairs Portage and down the face of a cliff. With a pack and a 125-pound Chestnut freight canoe on my back, and using notched poles for a ladder, I had been maneuvering so as not to slip and fall into the tops of the great pine trees below. Suddenly I realized that although this wasn't exactly a situation for relaxation, I needed a smoke. On reaching into my pocket, I found that in rolling my canoe down, the gunnel had hit my thigh and had broken the stem of my pipe.

With the roar of the waterfalls above and below, I let down the pack and looked mournfully at my injured friend. Certainly there is nothing more useless than a pipe with the wooden part of the stem broken. It leaks. You can't draw. In other words, you can't smoke. This called for a major conference.

Oscar Boyer, my French-Canadian guide, looked at it for a long time, and then we started in to search for mending materials. An old piece of a snowshoe which one of the men had picked up as a souvenir en route was placed in the water under a rock to soak while we boiled tea and prepared our lunch. After lunch we searched through the knitted rawhide until we found a thin piece. This we scraped paper-thin and, splinting the fractured stem with some birchbark, we wrapped the leather around the stem with a half-hitch at the end; and as the rawhide slowly dried by the fire, it contracted with great force, as rawhide will. To our delight, the device worked. That was one of the finest smokes I ever had. Oscar had discovered some tobacco to replenish our dwindling supply in a little pile over near the waterfall. Here the Indians down through the ages had left an offering to the Wina-Ba-Shoo of the falls and Shaking Mountain. Thus conciliated, the prankish and powerful woods spirit would let them pass in peace and not cause them to trip and fall off the portage trail, upset in the rapids, be sucked into the falls or harm them in the many other ways the Wina-Ba-Shoo knew, if he were displeased. . . .

The old pipe brought back fond memories, and in spite of the swirl of a busy city all around me, I was far away. I relaxed, and suddenly I looked up to see my old friend Tom Posey standing by my desk with a smile on his face, and the world was good again.

Tom wanted to run over to Marshall Field's Men's Grill for a sandwich. We were soon walking through the dreary February

weather amid the roar of the Loop traffic and the hurrying thousands. When we found ourselves snugly hidden away in a quiet
corner of the Grill over a cup of coffee, I told Tom what I had
been dreaming about. Tom had never been in the North country,
but one thing led to another and before we knew it, we were making grub lists, equipment lists—and so another wilderness trip was
born. For the next seven months we had great fun planning and
getting ready.

And so another wilderness trip was born! This particular one
grew out of a "pipe dream" and the meeting of two old friends—
my pipe and my friend Tom. Or, maybe it was the good spirits
that wafted down on the north wind that day from some hidden
lake to lure me back and to bring my friend so that he too could
become an addict of glowing birch logs, the wind in the pines, and
the fragrant smell of the balsam.

> It came again today in an unexpected way,
> A heart tug and a tinglin' of the spine;
> A symphony too high and clear for the ordinary ear,
> Like a soft breeze in the branches of a pine.
>
> From a land still locked in snow, came a message soft
>   and low,
> A spirit voice a thousand miles away;
> Dim trails and lakes are there and the Deer and Moose
>   and Bear,
> The call has come. I start my plans today.